CRITICAL ESSAYS:
Achebe, Baldwin, Cullen, Ngugi, and Tutuola

Sydney E. Onyeberechi

ISBN: 1-890279-79-X

Rising Star Publishers

What people are saying about the book:

Critical Essays . . . is a very welcome critical intervention and explanatory hermeneutics, whose great strength lies in Dr. Sydney Onyeberechi's probing critical insights into the works he has chosen to study and explain; the thematic strands which he elaborates through these works; the refreshing new readings of Achebe, Baldwin, and Ngugi; the sanguine reevaluation of Amos Tutuola; and the gallant defense of Countee Cullen against his unwarranted demonization even by persons unfamiliar with his writing. In the end, the author enables us to see these canonical Black writers in "new", even populist lights. Because Dr. Onyeberechi writes about subjects with which he is most familiar, readers of *Critical Essays* will also be pleasantly impressed by his authority and confidence.

--Dubem Okafor, Ph.D.
Professor of English, African, & World Literatures,
Kutztown University of Pennsylvania

CRITICAL ESSAYS:
Achebe, Baldwin, Cullen, Ngugi, and Tutuola

Sydney E. Onyeberechi

Rising Star Publishers

Hyattsville, Maryland, U.S.A.

Published by
Rising Star Publishers
2105 Amherst Road
Hyattsville, MD 20783
Tel.: 301-422-2665
FAX: 301-422-2720
or
P. O. Box 7413
Langley Park, MD 20787

Printed and produced in the United States of America.

Library of Congress Cataloging-in-Publication Data

Onyeberechi, Sydney.
    Critical essays : Achebe, Baldwin, Cullen, Ngugi, and Tutuola /
Sydney E. Onyeberechi.
        P.   cm.
    ISBN 1-890279-79-X pb
    1. Africa literature (English)--History and criticism.
    2. American literature--Afro-American authors--history and
criticism.   3. Cullen, Countee, 1903-1946--Criticism and
interpretation.   4. Ngugi wa Thiong'o, 1938- --Criticism and
interpretation.   5. Baldwin, James, 1924- --Criticism and
interpretation. ، 6. Achebe, Chinua--Criticism and interpretation.
    7. Tutuola, Amos--Criticism and interpretation.   8. Afro-Americans
in literature.   9. Nigeria--In literature.   10. Kenya--In
literature.; 1. Title.
    PR9340 . 069 1999   99-33351
    820 . 9 ' 96--dc21   CIP

Library of Congress Catalog Card Number: 99-74271

Cover design by Martin Ebube
Text typesetting and design by Obi Harrison Ekwonna

ISBN: 1-890279-79-X

10 9 8 7 6 5 4 3 2 1

Dedication:

This book is affectionately dedicated to my dear wife, Francisca and our three sons, Chinedu, Onyeali and Odunze.

About the Author:

Sydney Emeh Onyeberechi, the first of five children by Stephen and Theresa Onyeberechi was born in Emekuku, Owerri, formerly in Eastern Nigeria. His father was a school teacher and gave him the benefit of early schooling. He had his primary school education at Our Lady's School, Emekuku his home town.

Before proceeding to the Teacher Training College at the Holy Ghost College, Umuahia, former Eastern Nigeria, he taught for three years as a "pupil teacher" under the Catholic Mission. After completing his studies at Umuahia and a few years of teaching in the school system of the former Eastern Nigeria Ministry of Education, he came to the United States to continue his education.

In 1970 and 1971 respectively, he was awarded B.A. and M. A. in English by the University of Oregon, where his poems appeared regularly in the *Oregon Daily Emerald*.

He was on the faculty of Virginia State University and taught Freshman Writing and African Literature (1972-1983) and resigned his appointment to commence his doctoral program at the University of Maryland, College Park, where he was awarded his Ph.D. (1986). Dr. Onyeberechi joined Morgan State University as a lecturer in September 1986 and is currently a tenured Assistant Professor of English. He is the author of *Africa: Melodies and Thoughts*, a book of poetry.

Table of Contents

Author's Preface:

As the subject matter of this preface is literature, it is functionally appropriate for us to attempt a working definition of literature in order for us to keep in perspective the characteristic functions of this all-important creation of the human imagination, as they relate to the works studied in this book, or rather as these functions manifest themselves in the works under discussion. This being said, literature then could be safely defined as an artistic literary expression of human experience within a given culture. It could be primarily entertaining, unobtrusively instructive, imaginatively probing and insightful, deliberately satiric, and ironically exhilarating and if need be, purposefully contentious, and at its best awesome and liberating to the readers as well as the characters involved. And for the benefit of the lone poetic work in this book, poetry though part of literature could be defined here as an artistic, literary distillation of consciousness whose subject matter is every human experience that the poets's imagination could grapple with. The five writers whose works are studied in this book (with the exception of Tutuola whose "critical acclaim" has been controversial since 1952—the date of his first book, *The Palm-Wine Drinkard*) are veteran authors whose literary accolades rest on solid foundations; whose works examined herein embody or manifest, in varying degrees, artistic expression of human experience in the various cultures of their settings and satisfy the functional corollaries of literature enunciated in the attempted definitions above.

This book opens with a defense of Countee Cullen, one of the finest American poets of the twentieth century by all accounts, but whose greatness and stature as a poet is nimbled at by some unrelenting critics--detractors, who refuse to consider the effective message (content), and craftsmanship of his poetry but hold fast to his occasional prose pronouncements that seem at odds with his real accomplishments for his people in particular, and humanity in general, as the sum total of his evaluation as a poet. One would think that in a matter of taste regarding medium and form, the artist is accorded the freedom of being the sole arbiter of his inclinations. To set a boundary for the artist's talent is to diminish the horizon of his subject matter, thereby gaging his creativity. The artist--the poet, to be specific in this case--is entitled to, and should exercise the corrective musings of self-doubt, if his veracity as a creative artist is to be ensured.

Countee Cullen, like any true artist, engaged in and articulated his self-questioning of the language, form and content of his craft. There is nothing wrong about this self-probing on the part of any artist. What should essentially be an issue is whether a particular artist has used his creativity to denigrate the humanity of those his work ought to uphold. Cullen is never guilty of this breach. What has created an apparently lingering blot on his reputation as a poet, in some quarters, is a misguided harp on his entitled self-questioning by early critics, like Benjamin Brawley whose scarlet--letter observation on Cullen's expressed views on his poetry is quoted and put in proper perspective on pages five and six of this book.

In their introduction to Countee Cullen's poetry in *The Norton Anthology of American Literature*. Volume 2, 1979, the editors have this to say:

> The poet Countee Cullen was one involved in the
> Harlem Renaissance who felt most sensitively the
> dilemma of responding to then traditional standards
> for poetic excellence while also expressing the
> distinctive experience of Afro-Americans. (142)

Nothing in the above quotation is or should be indicting of Countee Cullen as a poet, or as member of a particular human group. In either capacity he is exercising his individual right to self-questioning, to the enigma of choice, in order for him to decide how best he could discharge his obligation to art and the human condition of his race. To perpetuate the notion that "Cullen is no good" (using the words of one of my freshman students, who rejected Countee Cullen from the list of African American poets the class was discussing), is a great disservice to the memory of a poet whose works are impeccable master-pieces, as well as compelling expressions of the dire circumstances man's inhumanity to man has put his people through.

On close questioning, the student revealed that he was quoting his high school teacher's reaction to Countee Cullen. That student's rote rejection of Cullen on the apparent prompting of his teacher supposedly based on the now hackneyed "dual allegiance" paradigm was seminal in this author's decision to proffer a defense on Cullen's behalf.

As we still live in a world where action speaks louder than words, Cullen's occasional prose self-questionings are his "words," his poetry--his copious poems which constitute his "action," should be a valid barometer of his commitment to his art and to his readership--his people, in particular, and humanity at large. Any other criteria of evaluation of this great poet would be extraneous and implausible.

From Cullen we come to another controversial author--controversial for quite different reasons. The author this time is Amos Tutuola, a Yoruba from Nigeria, whose publication of his first novel, *The Palm-Wine Drinkard* in 1952, gave him the fateful notoriety of being the first Nigerian novelist to publish in English. Unlike Cullen, a scholar and polished poet, whose measured prose utterances concerning his dilemma about which poetic route to follow, was the bone of contention against him by some of his contemporaries, the row for and against Tutuola emanated from a wounded pride on the part of some of his country men and women, and paternalistic eagerness to over praise and generalize the exotic and mediocre on the part of Western literary critics of works coming out of Africa.

The initial resentment against Tutuola by some Nigerians centered around his level of education--(he only completed Standard Six), and his ungrammatical use of English Language which some of his learned country men and women regarded as a national disgrace. They considered his audacity to write in English in the first place, and his being heralded as a trail blazer a national insult. Tutuola would not go away even when he was being described as a mere reporter or transcriber and not the creative genius of the stories he has written. But now Tutuola's reputation as a writer is firmly established in his own country after he has published novel after novel drawing from the same tested source--the Yoruba folklore and proved that his creativity was not a fluke. Even critics like Sunday O. Anozie, who would not concede anything to Tutuola's talent as a writer, does acknowledge the beneficial import of the events narrated in Tutuola's stories:

> Tutuola's world . . . is a disturbed world, prelogical and sometime crepuscular, in which, moreover, events take place by themselves without any logical, intellectual connection. Nevertheless, in traditional African society, these are events which, in the . . . context of the collective consciousness, provide an ethical perspective and constitute an efficacious means of education. (*Research in African Literatures*. Vol. 4, No. 1: 239-240)

Granted that Tutuola's folklore and mythological world is a dim world of bafflements and surprises, our interest in *The Palm-Wine Drinkard*, as revealed in our discussion in this book, is focused on how Tutuola is able to fuse events and adventures to satisfy the didactic and ethical demands of folkloric works. Specifically, "Myth, Magic and Appetite . . . ," the title of our study in *Critical Essays* discusses how Tutuola uses the wealth of his Yoruba folklore to weave some incredible, mesmerizing stories (*The Palm-Wine Drinkard* is made up of stories within a story), to inform and entertain his readers, and at the same time warn them against unbridled appetite and unattainable desires.

In this novel Tutuola employs the technique of direct narration. He lets us hear from the protagonist--the palm-wine drinkard, himself. This character and narrator of his own story is unabashed in his confession. He introduces himself as a man with abnormal appetite for palm-wine "who drank two hundred and twenty-five kegs of palm-wine in a day during his heydays" (*Critical Essays* 13-14). This must be a shocker to the reader, but he must learn to suspend doubts and follow the drinkard's story with unflagging attention, if he (the reader) is to imbibe the ethical and educational lessons intended by the drinkard's bizarre escapades later on in the novel. The drinkard must not be allowed to squander his life in drinking orgies with his friends. He has to be rescued; his "bagnio panders"--his father and his palm-wine tapster must be expunged from his life through natural attrition. The sudden deaths of these two procurers of palm-wine for the drinkard has left him bewildered and without friends.

When he leaves his father's hometown one morning to find his dead tapster, we would not see him again in the world of human beings until the ten-year period of his mythical expedition is over with some qualified successes—"qualified" because his tapster, the expressed object of his mission, could not return to the drinkard's home town with him. However, the drinkard has scored some successes for himself--he is wiser; at least he has learned that death is a finality, and he has done some civic good in his evolved capacity as a mythical hero both in his adventures in the under-world of demonic adversaries and eventually in his ingenuity in helping to banish famine in his home town.

In conclusion, this chapter takes the reader on a critical tour of the different episodes of the novel, and provides a comprehensive synthesis of the drinkard's motives, actions and adventures in the context of the novel's African setting, to lighten the reader's task of making meaning of this Nigerian maiden novel in English. We are encouraged to be mindful of the drinkard's regenerative metamorphosis in the novel, and also not to minimize Tutuola's "facility in the use of English he evolved for himself, to bring us the cultural intelligence of his people (African in general, and Yoruba in particular) from the dim recesses of mythical past" (25).

We leave Tutuola's palm-wine drinkard and his world of make-believe and turn to Achebe's history-recreating fiction, *Arrow of God*, in the third chapter of *Critical Essays*. It is relevant to our discussion to point out at the onset that *Things Fall Apart*, *No Longer at Ease*, and *Arrow of God* constitute a trilogy of tragic novels by Chinua Achebe, whose main characters: Okonkwo, Obi, and Ezeulu, the chief priest of Ulu, are catapulted unto societal greatness by their individual capabilities and public trust, but are all brought down by their unyielding self-pride and self-imposed moral blindness to the shifting protocols and demands of their times. "Superstition and the Riddle of Power . . ." highlights the contradictions in Achebe's portrayal of Ezeulu the stalwart character of *Arrow of God*, thereby ensuring his eventual downfall in the novel.

Ezeulu is presented to us as the Chief Priest of the Deity Ulu, the protector of Umuaro clan; in this capacity, he has enormous spiritual power over his people and is no doubt devoted to his duties to his deity and the people of Umuaro. At the same time, he is shown to be a man who is gloatingly aware of this power and would not mind pushing the envelop to test if it is real. It is his disposition to verify this power that hastens the demise of his authority and relevance in Umuaro clan and constitutes the riddle of power in *Arrow of God*. Oladele Taiwo puts it succinctly thus:

> [Ezeulu] is the possessor of spiritual authority and, with it, some temporal power. An outstanding religious leader, he manifests great skill in the manipulation of men and events. But he is also ambitious and arrogant. It is important to bear in mind Ezeulu's strengths and weaknesses for, without this knowledge, one cannot truly appreciate the various forces which bring about his isolation and the magnitude of the disaster which results from his fall. (132)

Critical Essays makes it clear that Ezeulu's strengths lie in his faithful execution of his religious duties for the benefit of his community and also in his recognition that his power is an invested one and not an absolute authority. Conversely, the Chief Priest's weaknesses reside in his inability to know the difference between him and Ulu, thereby arrogating to himself the power of the deity. Again, Taiwo elucidates:

> We meet him here in a position of strength, waiting patiently to be able to perform the vital functions of announcing the arrival of the new moon. We see from the beginning the tremendous influence and authority he has on the fate of his people. When later in the novel this immense authority is misapplied, the people suffered untold hardship. (133)

Surely, Umuaro clan suffered greatly when Ezeulu, out of misplaced feeling of vengeance against his people, refused to consume the remaining yams he ought to have eaten, and announces the date of the New Yam Festival, to clear the way for the people to harvest their yams. But by his refusal to perform the ritual that gave validity to his office, Ezeulu invariably made his role as the Chief Priest irrelevant. (Here lies superstition and the riddle of power.)

Having taken us through the vista of Ezeulu's animistic religion with its riddling atmosphere, and the Chief Priest's self-imposed isolation, *Critical Essays* launches us on a satirical probe of "the puritanical hypocrisy and cultural smugness [of] the Christian religion and its agents" (Kalu Ogbaa *CLA* 171) that have made John Grimes and his likes allegorical orphans in their father's mansion. John Grimes is the protagonist and partial narrator of James Baldwin's *Go Tell It on The Mountain*. He is the bastard son of Elizabeth, the second wife of Gabriel Grimes, the deacon of "The Temple of the Fire Baptized."

In this novel, Baldwin achieves a multi-faceted objective: he wants us to see John as an indomitable spirit whose quest for salvation is unstoppable, not even by Gabriel's obstructionist and loveless demeanor towards him; he also unveils Gabriel's religious hypocrisy, which is analogous to America's vaunted moral leadership; Baldwin is also engaging in a one-man non-violent protest to inform and reform himself and his country men and women so that they could live and let live. As we read *Go Tell It on the Mountain*, we must not lose sight of fine women like Deborah, Esther and Elizabeth--women who were used and discarded by "holy" Gabriel, whose only outlook on life is to protect himself from the glare of public scrutiny by wrapping himself with the aura of false religiosity.

Whatever is our angle of approach in this novel, James Baldwin insists that we recognize this young man as "a metaphor of resilience and inspiration for the oppressed and abused and bewildered by the cruel environmental predicaments beyond their knowledge and control" (*Critical Essays* 44).

We must not categorize John Grimes' loveless family circumstance as black ghetto problem. To do this is to be heedless of Kalu Ogbaa's admonition that "the black America's problems are

America's . . . that must be solved by all Americans" (*CLA* 172). This solution will only be achieved by inclusive love and untrammeled equity.

Throughout human history–biblical or secular, man has preoccupied himself with the intrinsic value of the land. For those who subscribe to Judeo-Christian faith and thereby to the scriptures, Adam and Eve, "our first parents," began their lives together in the Garden of Eden, a contractual place God had given them for their abode and comfort here on earth, as long as they would remain in a state of pristine innocence. Other religions of the world have their own different versions of how man's entitlement to the land emanated from Divine Ordinance. Even some human groups who have cruelly displaced and almost wiped out original inhabitants of certain regions of the world have claimed "Manifest Destiny," that is, a Divine sanction for their occupation of the land. Wars after wars have been fought, are being fought, and will be fought over territories–land, and individuals will continue to be the victims.

It is this veneration of, and claim to the land that James Ngugi, now Ngugi wa Thiong'o, of Kenya, used as the backdrop of his first novel, *Weep Not, Child* (1964). The child being consoled in the title is of-course, Njoroge, the fateful idealist and protagonist of the novel, whose world crashes around him because of his people's resolve to retrieve the land that was stolen from them by British Settlers in pre-Independence Kenya.

The novel's central focus is on the need for Njoroge to acquire education in order to enable his family, and the Kenyan people, to get back their land. In this novel the author is describing in no unmistakable terms, the cruelty and devastations the Kenyan people suffered in the hands of British settlers–then-turned colonial officials. Ngugi, as it were, in this his maiden novel, poses some unresolvable questions to all of us: First, why should a people whose religious faith is based on Divine Ordinance of the land to man be so insensitive as to deny other peoples such religious and cultural belief in their ownership of their own land? This is a logical question because for the Kenyans of *Weep Not, Child*, Murungu, (the Creator), caused a holy tree to sprout and grow taller and taller. Then he made the first man, Gikuyu, and the first woman, Mumbi, and commanded them to cultivate the land for their upkeep, only to offer him periodical sacrifices under his sacred tree. It is with this background that the Mau Mau Resistence Movement of the 1950's--a fierce battle to retrieve the land in the novel, could make sense.

Another question that Ngugi is asking is why Ngotho, Njoroge's father, should be a share-cropper on the land that would normally belong to him. Of course, we now know why after reading the novel: "Mr. Howlands, a British settler now owned the land that belonged to Njoroge's ancestors" (*Critical Essays* 47). At this juncture we are prompted to ask our own series of questions about this audacity: Is it right ? Is it ethical? Is it just? Ngugi gives no clean-cut answers to our musings. Finally, he puts before us a very difficult question to resolve: What is the best instrument of retrieving the land–the non-violent route of formal education, idealistically chosen by Njoroge, the protagonist, or the Mau-Mau's approach?

From what has taken place in the novel, we can only make some inferential conclusions after stacking the cards. At the end of the novel all adversaries–the major contestants, Mr. Howlands and his Kenyan uncle Tom, Chief Jacobo; Ngotho and his two sons and many, many ordinary people have all become casualties. Only Njoroge and his two mothers (his father had two wives), his mother and Njeri remain the sole survivors. Perhaps, Ngugi ends the novel on this dismal note in order to teach Njoroge and others like him an enduring lesson: that in the people's fight for their land and cultural identity, indifference or mere idealism is self-destructive.

Chapter six, is devoted to *Things Fall Apart*, Achebe's master stroke. It is a natural tendency of readers, especially the Western, to develop a grudging reading of foreign novels. This tendency is even more pronounced among American College students, who cringe at any reading assignments that have foreign components. Many teachers of literature that have talked to this writer attest to this same experience with their students. However, all of these teachers, without exception, say that this antipathy on the part of their students, is not extended to any of Achebe's novels. On being asked why this is so, the consensus is that Achebe's novels are self-motivating; they bait the readers' interest. Of course, what my professional colleagues are referring to here, is Achebe's effective use of suspense–the taste bud of successful fiction, to galvanize his readers.

Achebe's demonstration of this fictional device in *Things Fall Apart* is the subject matter of this chapter appropriately titled, "Suspense of Motif in Achebe's Things Fall Apart. Here, Achebe's calculated dribble in presenting the major actions of the novel is persuasively highlighted for the readers' attention. We are made to understand that this "calculated dribble"–the art of giving only "measured information at strategic intervals . . ." (58), is the glue that binds the major actions of the novel together, as affirmed in this observation:

> Whether we are anticipating Okonkwo's self-destruction, or Umuofia's killing of Ikemefuna, or the cleavage between Nwoye and his father, or the eventual conflict between the missionaries and Umuofia . . . (56)

the present writer sees "the major actions of the novel [as] one string effectively held together by the unifying mnemonics of suspense" (55-56). This is Achebe's master stroke, his ability not to bore the reader with loaded information, by engaging in artful sparsity and giving strategic clues to aid the reader's memory and ensure zestful anticipation. The chapter identifies these "strategic clues" and discusses how they, severally, create the fictional tapestry that makes *Things Fall Apart* a spell-binding novel.

The next chapter takes me back down memory lane. To have seen James Baldwin, in person, is cherished by this writer as a phenomenal privilege and practical lesson in artistic fearlessness and messianic commitment to writing, as a means of effecting change in society. The encounter happened in 1980 at the Annual Conference of African Literature Association in Gainesville, Florida. We had received prior announcement that Baldwin and Achebe would be at the Conference to address and chat with the members. Some of us did not take this notice seriously; we thought it was a ploy to galvanize attendance. But it was not. It was awesome for some of us who were seeing these literary stalwarts of our century for the first time. It was magic! Achebe, himself, records his own recollections of their auspicious meeting at the Conference, in the chapter entitled "Postscript: James Baldwin (1924–1987)" in his book, *Hopes and Impediments* in (1989). He recalls the zestful applause of welcome accorded to Baldwin and himself by the Association, as they entered the hall, and how Baldwin was in a felicitous mood, dispensing his characteristic goodwill to all (174).

What happened minutes into Baldwin's opening statements is the reason for this historical preamble. As Baldwin was rewarding his audience with anecdotal pleasantries, a misguided voice came through the inter-com brazen with racial slurs on him and Achebe. Anyone who has studied the psychology of racial intimidation would know that the sole aim of the racist interloper was to disrupt the Conference and deny its members the beneficial insights of these two literary sages in their midst. But the "voice" was as ephemeral as it was sudden and did not achieve its demoniacal intention. Something intended to becloud the Conference, or even disband such illustrious gathering of scholars, writers and thinkers of all persuasions ended up being one of the ennobling chapters in its annals. This conversion of hateful intent into strength was partly due to the poised integrity of these two indomitable writers of our time, and partly due to Baldwin's unsparing frankness in addressing the blatant racial insult on their persons.

This "unsparing frankness", this "poised integrity" in confronting such a patent assault on human inalienable dignity and rights, is the subject matter of chapter seven of *Critical Essays*. Baldwin's sincerity and scorching, yet affable use of language to expose the shortcomings of his society, to make it fair and whole for all its citizens, is studied in this chapter. In "Satiric Candor in *The Fire Next Time*" the title of this chapter, we are made aware of "the abiding role of a satirist or social critic, [which] is to infuse understanding and the exercise of common sense in his audience, his readers" (75). Believing that knowledge is power, Baldwin finds it necessary to engage in compulsive revelations in order to arm his nephew with this power. His nephew has to be made aware of the unjust heritage into which he is born. However, while Baldwin is bristling in his attack on his nation for its vaunted sermon on human rights, he is tempered in his directives to his nephew about the course of action he must take in his battle to retrieve and repair his stolen and battered heritage. He categorically admonishes him to overpower that "enemy" with love. This is the thrust of *The Fire Next Time*. Let us hope that all sections of America, and indeed, all sections of humanity, including that hateful voice in Gainesville, Florida, would mend their ways in order for us to avoid pulling down the nihilistic conflagration implied in the title of Baldwin's work.

The final chapter of this preface, "Contrapuntal Characters in Achebe's *Things Fall Apart*" is of particular interest, because it implicitly invokes two primary functions of art: entertainment and instruction. In the golden age of the African family, of the kindred, of the village, there were frequent cultural and moral orientations by the head of the family, by the oldest man in the kindred, who held the "Ofo," the totem instrument of kindred authority, and by the itinerant bards, who by virtue of their calling served as moral and cultural custodians. As these cultural dynamics are no longer intact or effective in our "modern" society, the present writer feels that the African contemporary writer has a commitment to fill the void. This is not a matter of choice but of duty.

Like his counterparts, past and present, elsewhere in the world, the African contemporary fiction writer is a story-teller, whose essential functions include entertaining his audience (readers) and at the same time enlightening them. Achebe whose maiden novel, *Things Fall Apart*, is a practical response to Joyce Cary's *Mr. Johnson*, a satirical novel on Nigeria and Nigerians, is very much aware of these two cardinal functions of fiction. In this his first novel, Achebe understands his responsibilities and executed them effectively. He is cognizant of the Igbo adage which stipulates that a "traveled child" is wiser and far-seeing than an old person, who never stirred out of doors. He also understands that in our time, the African writer is that traveled child, that by his vocation and insight–his intellectual travel (the art of fiction writing is a journey of the mind and intellect to boundless limits of imagination and perception), he must of necessity satisfy the enjoyment as well as the dialectic function of story telling. Achebe embraces this understanding without any apology and without sacrificing artistic "objectivity." He writes:

> I would be quite satisfied if my novels (especially the
> ones I set in the past) did no more than teach my
> readers that their past . . . with all its imperfections .
> . . was not one long night of savagery from which the
> first Europeans acting on God's behalf delivered
> them. (*Hopes and Impediments* 45)

The author of *Things Fall Apart* masterfully succeeds in
shattering the myth contained in the above observation.   His
contrapuntal utilization of characters works to his advantage of
unobtrusively enlightening his readers and at the same time achieving
objectivity in his presentation of ideas.   This   juxtaposition of
contraries in the portrayal of his characters enables Achebe's readers
to "see" and hear the characters without editorial commentaries.
Through the unmediated actions and utterances of paired characters
like Okonkwo and his best friend Obierika; Okonkwo and Unoka, his
father; Okonkwo and Nwoye, his son; Akunna, an Umuofia elder and
Mr. Brown, the white missionary, we get a clear picture of their
differences and laugh at their obduracies and ignorance of each
other's protocol. As readers, literary scholars and critics, we should
be thankful to the writers--"traveled children" in our midst whose
sensibilities and art of story-telling probe the intricate tapestry
(ourselves) we call humankind, for our necessary amusement and
edification.

As we come to the end of this preface, it is hoped that the
reader has been given ample and impelling overview to urge and
sustain his/her interest in *Critical Essays* and its subject matter. The
chapters of this book were read by me at several conferences
including College Language Association (CLA), Middle Atlantic
Writers Association (MAWA), National Council of Teachers of
English (NCTE), and the Zora Neale Hurston Society. The book's
thematic approach and incisive discussions would make it an
invaluable companion to students and teachers of literature and
humanities.

Works Cited

Achebe, Chinua. *Hopes and Impediments: Selected Essays*. New York: Doubleday, 1989.

Anozie, Sunday O. "Amos Tutuola: Literature and Folklore, or The Problem of Synthesis" printed in *Research in African Literatures*.

Gottesman, Roland. et al. editors, *The Norton Anthology of American Literature*. Volume 2, New York: W. W. Norton and Company, 1979.

Ogbaa, Kalu. "Protest and The Individual Talents of Three Black Novelists." *CLA Journal*. Volume xxxv, Number 2, (December 1991): 159-184.

Taiwo, Oladele. *Culture and the Nigerian Novel*. New York: St. Martin's Press, 1976.

Sydney E. Onyeberechi, Morgan State University, 1999

Chapter One

In Defense of Cullen's Dual Allegiance

C ountee Cullen is a poet that should be approached with rare objectivity if he is to be accorded his due merit as a poetic genius. This objectivity is only achieved when the execution and the message of Cullen's poetry is appreciated with unbiased disposition, not withstanding Cullen's overt expression, which has lent itself to detracting connotations. We have to appreciate Cullen as a poet of two camps, and these two camps shared his artistic allegiance throughout his career. As should be expected, this split vision over form and responsibility, created a persistent dilemma in the young poet. His vision of art, as "a scholar and lover of traditional literature," (Arthur Davis 73) is conventional in form. On the other hand, even though he resented, "the urgings from within and without that tried to make him a Negro poet" (Davis 73), Cullen must have realized subconsciously that he had a responsibility to his race. This awareness is reflected in the titles and content of his poems, which will be considered later in this paper.

Cullen was quite aware of his dual stewardship in his poetry.

He had, on several occasions, articulated his dilemma. Resenting attempts to limit his creative freedom as a poet, he wrote:

> Must we, willy-nilly, be forced into writing nothing
> but the old atavistic urges, the more savage and none
> too beautiful aspects of our lives? May we not chant
> to the Sun-god, if we will, create a bit of phantasy in
> which not a spiritual or a blues appears . . . ? (*The
> Crisis*. Nov. 1929: 373. Quoted by Davis *From the
> Dark Tower* 1974: 73.)

The message carried in this phrase, "and none too beautiful aspects of our lives," is heavily contrasted by the fourth stanza of Cullen's "A Song of Praise":

> My love is dark as yours is fair,
> Yet lovelier I hold her
> Than listless maids with pallid her
> and blood that's thin and colder. (*On These I Stand* 4)

Cullen himself explains it all in this statement he released to the New York Times, December 2, 1923, and quoted by Margaret Perry in her *A Bio-Bibliography of Countee P. Cullen, 1903-1946*:

> In spite of myself, however, I find that I am actuated
> by a strong sense of race consciousness. This grows
> upon me, I find, as I grow older. And although I
> struggle against it, it colors my writing, I fear, in spite
> of everything I can do. (6)

Showing the other side of his poetic coin, Countee Cullen expressed it in this view, "Most things I write, I do for the sheer love of the music in them." (Quoted by Perry 16, from Jay Saunders Redding's *To Make a Poet Black* 109). Cullen's pull toward traditional poetry was motivated not only by "the sheer love of music." It was his desire to leave aspirations, his "ecstasy" in some polished forms to endure the passage of time. In his own words, it is to "leave something so written to after times as they should not willingly let it die." (Quoted by Don M. Wolfe in the "Forward" of Perry's *A Bio-Bibliography xiii*).

Commenting on Cullen's conventional preference and the amount of work that went into his art, Blanch Ferguson wrote:

> . . . he preferred conventional form. He often said that poetry came out of him "metered and rhymed." His poems were proof of this, and he was good. He was proud, too, of the diligence that had forced him to rewrite each line until it was as perfect as he could make it. (49)

This diligent craftsmanship is evidenced in his lyric poem, "Advice to Beauty." A stanza of this poem is quoted below:

> Beauty beats so frail a wing
> Suffer men to gaze, poets to sing
> How radiant you are, compare
> And favor you that more rare
> Bird of delight: a lovely face
> Matched with an equal inner grace. (Ferguson 59)

The above stanza, inspired by Sydonia Byrd, could have been written by John Keats or any of his contemporaries. Cullen's adroitness and precision in conventional poetry is further revealed in the stanza that follows below. On his first trip with his father in 1926, Countee Cullen was fascinated by the placid blueness of the Mediterranean Sea. To express his awe at the mystic hue of the sea, Cullen pressed his love of conventional poetry into service. He wrote, as transcribed by Ferguson in her book on Cullen:

> Only the hand that never erred
> Bent on beauty, created--spurred,
> Could mix and mingle such a dye,
> Nor leave its like in earth or sky. (71)

In the lines just quoted, we feel the grasp of Cullen's talent for sophistication and mellow imagery, and his powerful use of rhyming couplets.

As a "preeminently lyric poet," it could be said that Cullen achieved his heart's desire in poetry--that of being "a rank conservative, loving the measured line and skillful rhyme" (Davis 75). Eugenia Collier attests to this praise in these words, "Countee Cullen's delicate sonnets of love and life are among the most beautiful produced by the American of his time" (*CLA Journal* 1967 *the quotation used here is from the reprint in Gibson 1973:71).

His former teacher of poetry, Robert S. Hillyer, wrote that Cullen,

> . . . was the first American poet to publish a poem in
> rime royal the difficult seven-line stanza made famous
> by Chaucer and Masefield. (Ferguson 58)

The above designation, an "American poet" must have satisfied Cullen, who once told a New York reporter, "I want to be known as a poet and not as a Negro poet." His affinity with Chaucer and Masefield in the above encomium is in keeping with his expressed philosophy about Negro poetry:

> As heretical as it may sound, there is the probability
> that Negro poets, dependent as they are on the English
> language, may have more to gain from the rich
> background of English and American poetry than
> from any nebulous atavistic yearning toward an
> African inheritance. (Quoted in *From the Dark Tower*,
> from Cullen's "Forward" to *Carolling Dusk* 1927)

Is it not ironic, therefore, that "there are critics who believe that his 'Heritage' a poem of African theme, is the best poem published during the Harlem Renaissance?"

This ambivalence predicates Cullen's career as a poet. It is to be emphasized, however, that his desire toward the mainstream in poetry is circumstantial. Being too much aware of the derogatory implication of the label "a Negro Poet," Cullen determined to fight the appendage. In his time, the label meant a crude "poet" with lesser talent for poetry. This type of "poet" was only to be regarded as a poet among his people. And only so, if he wrote about the life of these "anthropological curiosities." Countee Cullen vehemently rejected this insult. He wanted to prove that "pure" art could reside in some people regardless of the color of their skin.

This was the circumstance that created his dual allegiance in poetry. It is to be put right, however, that Cullen never rejected the "Negroness" in him. What he rejected was the tradition that made stereotypes of Negroes. He was too much of that race to shun its experience and problems in America. His upbringing in the house of his adoptive father, Reverend Frederick Cullen of Harlem, made it virtually impossible for Cullen to be insensitive to the trepidations of his race in the America of his time. How could he, while the rectory of his father's church was "the center of Harlem's reaction to racial violence across the country?" As Alan Shucard succinctly put it, "there was no avoiding black awareness in the rectory of that church, and there was no wish to avoid it" (9). Cullen in a way, gave testimony to this assertion when he said this about his poetry:

> . . . I find my poetry of itself treating of the Negro, of
> his joys and his sorrows--mostly of the latter and of
> the heights and depths of emotions I feel as a Negro.
> (*New York Times* December 2, 1923, reprinted in
> Perry's *A Bio-Bibliography* 1971: 16)

This unobtrusive revelation of the Negro (black) experience that Cullen hinted at, above, is what Stephen Henderson has termed "saturation" (10), an important requisite in Black poetry. It is ironic that in expressing these "heights and depths of emotions," Cullen achieved complementarity in form and content that has plagued criticism of his works by Negro critics. Writing on Cullen in *The Negro Genius*, Benjamin Brawley commented:

> . . . One might suppose that he would be treated with
> McKay and Hughes, but his sympathies, unlike theirs,

are with tradition and convention. In some lines he said that he wished his work to be judged on its merit, 'with no racial consideration to bolster it up.' Something of this cleavage runs through all that he has written and gives it an artificiality, a thinness of substance, of which one is not conscious in his two compeers.

I would say that Brawley is too hard on Cullen. After all, Countee Cullen was a dominant poet of the Harlem Renaissance. In this capacity he powerfully articulated in his own way, the brash inequities the Negro American experienced in his own native country. The phrase "in his own way," is very significant in understanding Cullen's "poetics." He must have realized very early in his career that we must not sing the blues or couch our life experiences in dialects to be "real", or authentic. Could there be a bolder and more powerful protest than these two lines of Cullen's poetry: "We shall not always plant while others reap / The golden increment of bursting fruit, . . . (Ferguson 90). It is interesting that not all Negro critics would dismiss Cullen as Brawley has done in his statement quoted above. Commenting on Cullen and the New Negro Renaissance, Ferguson has this to say:

> Countee's was one of the young voices making themselves heard in what was now being called the Negro Renaissance. A new spirit had begun to permeate the masses, and a new crop of writers emerged as their spokesmen. These young people believed that the day of the Negro stereotype . . . the grinning, shuffling, indolent clown was over. (91)

Margaret Perry describes Countee Cullen as a poet, a scholar, and a man "committed to helping his race achieve greater significance in American life" (xvi). Houston Barker's comment on Cullen's behalf among contemporary readers is a timely rescue:

> . . . If he is judged and sentenced to exile on the basis

of his aesthetic, a number of excellent statements on
the Black artist's task and difficulty are lost . . . He
wrote a number of outstanding romantic lyrics and
contributed racial poems that will endure because they
grant insight into Black American dilemma. (Baker
52)

In spite of his dual allegiance (the reason for which I have explained
earlier), Countee Cullen is a great poet. Arthur Davis describes him
as, "if not the finest, certainly one of the best poets of the New Negro
Renaissance" (Davis 75). Davis goes on to say this about Cullen:

As a poet Countee Cullen will probably outlast his
century. Measured by any standard, his work,
particularly the 'color' pieces, will be read as long as
protest poems have meaning in America. (81)

As I said earlier, Cullen achieved a beautiful fusion of form
and content, and used it effectively in his poetry that deals with racial
concerns. He put his "quatrains, couplets, stanzas of varying lengths,
and sonnets," to ironic use. With these he unleashed some of the
most powerful, yet subtle racial protests in America. What made his
brand of protest effective was that it compellingly appealed to
conscience. Writing on Cullen's type of protest, Davis said:

Cullen's protest poetry . . . was seldom, if ever, a
frontal attack. He preferred the oblique, the hinted,
the ironic approach. (79) Cullen had the skill of
McKay, but not the intensity. He preferred the
suggested to the blunt statement. He pricked rather
than slashed. (81)

A brief look at some of his poems will reveal how he put
conventional poetry to contemporary use. Let us consider his poem,
"Incident," for example:

Once riding in Old Baltimore,

Heart-filled, head-filled with glee,
I saw a Baltimorean
Keep looking straight at me.

Now I was eight and very small
And he was no whit bigger,
And so I smiled, but he poked out,
His tongue and called me 'Nigger.'

I saw the whole of Baltimore
From May until December
Of all the things that happened there
That's all that I remember. (Cullen 9)

In the above poem, the memory of the "Nigger" incident is made an object of art. Each of the unassailable quatrain stanzas is a capsule of information. But who would fail to realize the embedded message in the poem? How a white boy of about eight years knew that a fellow black boy of the same age was a "Nigger." The ironic angle of the poem is that the burden of explanation rests with the white parents of the boy. The poet got his message through, without any rumbles in his language.

Has any other Negro poet written a poem like "Yet do I Marvel" . . . a sonnet written with conventional precession? This poem of great ironic insight into the psychology of racial discrimination in America is a marvel to this writer. I am yet to read anything that approximates Cullen's under-current expression of the dilemma of the Negro poet, as conveyed in the final rhyming couplet of the poem: "Yet do I marvel at this curious thing: / To make a poet Black, and bid him sing" (Cullen 3). If these two lines are interpreted out of context (as some critics are inclined to do), one might insinuate the impression that what Cullen is suggesting is that black people are incapable of writing poetry. This is not what he means in these lines; he and other black poets of his time had demonstrated beyond doubt, the black man's creative ability in poetry. Rather, what Cullen is ironically demolishing in these two lines is the blind racial debate over the humanity of black people. Eugenia Collier's comment on these two lines unmasks the irony intended by Cullen in these lines, "I do not marvel, Countee Cullen, that God should bid the black poet sing - For who else could sing so well, and who else has such song" (Collier *CLA Journal* reprint in Gibson 83)? By implication, Cullen is saying all of these, and more.

My next example is another sonnet, "From the Dark Tower." I would like to quote it whole, because of the light it throws on the role Cullen played in the race struggle:

> We shall not always plant while others reap
> The golden increment of bursting fruit,
> Not always countenance, abject and mute,
> That lesser men should hold their brothers cheap;
> Not everlasting while others sleep
> Shall we beguile their limbs with mellow flute
> Not always bend to some more subtle brute;
> We were not made eternally to weep.
>
> The night whose sable breast relieves the stark,
> White stars is no less lovely being dark,
> And there are buds that cannot bloom at all
> In light, but crumble, piteous, and fall;
>
> So in the dark we hide the heart that bleeds,
> And wait, and tend our agonizing seeds. (Cullen 49)

This effective, subtle expression of Black economic oppression in America is yet to be paralleled by any other Black poet. Note the hope carried by the final couplet and the determination of the first two lines of the poem. Collier, who sees this poem as, "effectively expressing the spirit of the Harlem Renaissance" (*CLA Journal* reprint in Gibson 72), gives an interesting analysis of it. She comments:

> The image of a person planting the seeds of labor, knowing even as he plants that 'others' will pluck the fruit, is a picture of the frustration which is so often

the Negro's lot...In his basic symbol, then, Cullen
expresses the crux of the protest [poetry] which so
flourished in the Harlem Renaissance. (Reprint in
Gibson 73)

Continuing her analysis of Cullen's poem, Collier affirms:

> With skill of an impressionist painter, the poet
> juxtaposes black and white into a canvas of brilliant
> contrasts. The night is pictured as being beautiful
> because it is dark--a welcome relief from the stark
> whiteness of the stars. The image suggests pride in the
> Negritude which became important in the Harlem
> Renaissance--the pride in the physical beauty of the
> black people, the Negro folk culture which enriched
> America, the strength which the Negro has earned
> through suffering. (Reprint in Gibson 74)

In much the same vein, "For a Lady I Know," a four-line urbane
poetry, gives its message more effectively than any soapbox oration
of race protest could give in its jaggared tone:

> She even thinks that up in heaven
> Her class lies late and snores,
> While poor Black cherubs rise at seven
> To do celestial chores. (Cullen 49)

Who would read "Simon the Cyrenian Speaks" without a shudder?
This ironic view of the Black man's role in Christianity speaks for
itself. The last three lines carry the message:

> I did for Christ alone
> What all of Rome could not have wrought
> With bruise of lash or stone. (Cullen 33)

This ironic implication of the above lines is underscored. Let the
world clearly know that the black man did more for the cause of

Christianity than those who would use it to oppress him and his race. Is this not the message of Cullen's poem? How could Cullen have used his poetry to further the black cause? Why then should he be disparaged?

I have gone this length to prove that what is regarded as a split allegiance in Countee Cullen's poetry is never a repudiation of his race or his origin. His overt expression, notwithstanding, anyone who reads his poem, "Heritage," objectively will notice a strain of painful nostalgia. But as a poet given to sophistication of language and mellow imagery, Cullen approaches his own nostalgia with emotional control. For him, therefore, the poem becomes a manful reconciliation of time and reality, of what is tenable and what is not. It is never a rejection of Africa. The first four lines of the fifth stanza reveal his magic for contending his painful nostalgia:

> All day long and night through,
> One thing only must I do:
> Quench my pride and cool my blood,
> Lest I perish in the flood. (Cullen 24)

In concluding this paper I have to reiterate my earlier statement, that Countee Cullen is a great poet. His poetry stand the test of time as one of the signature tunes of the Harlem Renaissance. Whether we read him as a conventional lyric poet, or as an African American poet, his four volumes of poetry (*Color; Copper Sun; The Black Christ;* and *Media*) are all impeccable reservoirs of artistic craftsmanship by any standards.

If he has not risen to the stature of John Keats, his mentor, his failure to do so may be conjected. After all, most of the imitative English poets of the late 18th and early 19th centuries received unquestionable renown. If he failed to write like Langston Hughes, the latter did not write like Cullen either. What matters is that both are great poets. For those who would "dump" Cullen on the grounds that he did not cringe in his poetry, it suffices to say, in Soyinka's cautionary parlance, that a tiger does not have to exhibit his tigertude to be a tiger.

WORKS CITED

Baker, Houston A. Jr. *A Many-Colored Coats of Dreams: The Poetry of Countee Cullen.* Detroit, Michigan: 1974.

Brawley, Benjamin. *The Negro Genius.*

Collier, Eugenia W. "I Do Not Marvel, Countee Cullen." *CLA Journal.* 1967: 73-87. Reprinted in Donald Gibson. ed., *Modern Black Poets: A Collection of Critical Essays.* Englewood Cliffs, New Jersey. Prentice-Hall, Inc., 1973.

Cullen, Countee. *On These I Stand: An Anthology of the Best Poems of Countee Cullen.* New York: Harper and Row, Publishers, 1947.

Davis, Arthur P. *From the Dark Tower: Afro-American Writers 1900-1960.* Washington, D.C.: Howard University Press, 1974.

Ferguson, Blanche. *Countee Cullen and the Negro Renaissance.* New York: Dodd, Meand Co., 1966.

Henderson, Stephen. *Understanding the New Black Poetry.* New York: William Morrow and Company, 1973.

Margaret, Perry. *A Bio-Bibliography of Countee P. Cullen 1903-1946.* Westport, Connecticut: Greenwood Publishing Corporation, 1971.

Shucard, Alan R. *Countee Cullen.* Boston: Twayne Publishers, 1984.

Chapter Two

Myth, Magic and Appetite in Amos Tutuola's
The Palm-Wine Drinkard

In *The Palm-Wine Drinkard*, Tutuola lets the central character, the drinkard, tell his own story. What we have here in this bizarre collection of folk-stories, is a narrator who is fully aware of himself, his failings and his limitations. This character has the capacity for self-indictment and the will to persevere in order to find solution to his shortcomings and eventually to absolve himself of community censure. As we follow the drinkard on his necessary journey of self-exploration and regeneration, we shall keep in mind his compelling reason (Appetite), his super-human exaggerations (Myth) and his personal fortifications for this daring adventure (Juju and magic).

As the story begins, the Palm-Wine Drinkard introduces himself to us as an incredibly abnormal character who drank two hundred and twenty-five kegs of palm-wine in a day during his heydays (7). The drinkard in making this self-confession is not apologetic at all; he has no reason to be. his father, the richest man in his town, provided him with 560,000 palm-trees on a nine-mile farmland, and procured a tapster to serve his appetite (7). From this initial profile, we perceive an impending problem for the drinkard. What would this gluttonous prodigy who does nothing but drink do, in the event of his father's death or that of his tapster? This question is important because by his own admission, the drinkard is suffering from inveterate indolence and insatiable appetite:

> But when my father noticed that I could not do any work more than to drink, he engaged an expert palm-wine tapster for me; he had no other work more than to tap palm-wine every day. (7)

In the above revelation, the father and the tapster represent the cultural past that gave the drinkard a sense of euphoric abundance which left him unprepared, lonely and dejected after the sudden deaths of those dual panderers. The drinkard captures his hopelessness after the facts in this manner:

> When it was early in the morning of the next day, I had no palm-wine to drink at all and throughout that day I felt not so happy as before; I was seriously sat down in my palour; but when it was the third day that I had no palm-wine at all, all my friends did not come to my house again, they left me there alone, because there was no palm-wine for them to drink. (8)

This abandonment of the drinkard by his friends, this "sudden inexplicable collapse of his world" (Moore 42) portends well for the drinkard as the story unfolds. Tutuola is not going to abandon his hero, nor would he depict him as a public spectacle, even though the drinkard has through his excessive and uncontrollable appetite violated the Yoruba cultural code of decency in eating and drinking. He is, in Yoruba language, an "Alaseju"--someone with unnatural appetite. The Igbos call such an addict, "Onye-Akpuria"--one with a long throat, who would not mind taking food or drink from demons. The implication here is obvious - death. However, as the drinkard is a fictional exaggeration, Tutuola does not have an immediate physical death in store for him. After all, the author is operating within the cultural framework of his environment - his region. Gladys Agbobiyi, herself a Yoruba, underscores the validity of this observation in her article in the *Nigeria Magazine* 1968), concerning the realm and content of Tutuola's works. She asserts that "those who know Yoruba mythology and understand Yoruba philosophy of life, life after death, the spirit world and different types of gods and their media" would appreciate Tutuola's message and inclinations. As the author who is telling his story from the "collective subconscious" of his culture, Tutuola is aware that his hero, the drinkard, at this initial stage of his existence in the story has offended cultural and even natural probabilities by his abnormal appetite for palm-wine and by his despicable indolence. Something must be done to redeem the drinkard, if his story would be worth telling for the benefit of folk edification. Tutuola perceives this expectation; he knows it. His awareness of his obligation in *The Palm-Wine Drinkard* and his qualification thereof are aptly enunciated by Gerald Moore thus:

> [Tutuola] has lived through his material before ever he sets it down; the many fragments of folk-lore, ritual and belief embedded in it, are not just things remembered, but things already experienced; they have all passed through the transmuting fire of an individual imagination and have been shaped for its ends. (43)

Yes, Tutuola has shaped his story and has a definite design for his incredible hero. He knows that a prolonged image of the drinkard as a "sucker"--a bum--would be culturally repugnant. The traditional society and culture that spurned his story was a proud and noble one. The drinkard, therefore, must be either ennobled or permanently hoisted up for public ridicule. Tutuola chooses the former, but he must, first of all, expunge the two pandering influences that bait the drinker's appetite for palm-wine. This explains the sudden deaths of

the drinkard's father and his tapster. Having been thus stripped of his
paternal security and starved of palm-wine--his only socializing live-
wire--the drinkard is no longer able and equipped to function in
normal, human environment. He is now ready for a regenerative
adventure, his opportunity to evolve from a mundane exaggeration to
a mythical figure and social hero towards the end of the book. The
drinkard must now travel to his apparently mythical underworld
through the bush--through the thick equatorial forest in search of his
dead tapster. To the reader, this venture in search of a dead tapster
may look foolish, untenable and weird, but to the drinkard it is real,
feasible, and logical. According to him, he has a valid and pressing
urgency for this undertaking: "When I saw that there was no palm-
wine for me again, and nobody could tap it for me,--so that I said that
I would find out where my palm-wine tapster who had died was" (9).
He has collected reliable intelligence report to guide his epic quest:
"Then I thought within myself that old people who were saying that
the people who had died in this world, did not go to heaven directly,
but they were living in one place somewhere in this world" (9).
Finally, he has made his decision to embark on a mythical expedition
to confront death in person in order to ransom his dead tapster:

> One fine morning, I took all my active juju and also
> my father's juju with me and I left my father's
> hometown to find out whereabouts was my tapster
> who had died. (9)

From this point on, the drinkard's story acquires a mythical
aurora; what started as a tale of bizarre and bloated appetite is now
taking shape as a redemptive mission--a spiritual quest. 0. R.
Dathorne, perceiving this evolving role-change for the drinkard,
observes that the journey to Deads Town in search of his dead palm-
wine tapster is an attempt to perpetuate the transient, to give to the
sensual, qualities of spiritual longevity" (96). As a fictional
exaggeration, the drinkard must be equipped with the necessary
capacities to sublimate his roles in the story he is destined to be a
mythical hero. He has the capacity to endure untold and unnatural
hardships--"I was traveling from bushes to bushes and from forests to

forests and sleeping inside it for many days and months, I was sleeping on the branches of trees, because spirits--were just like partners, and to save my life from them; and again I could spend two or three months before reaching a town or a village" (9). To the reader, who does not understand the setting of Tutuola's story, the drinkard's mode of fortification and his decision to make the bush, forest the theater of his mythical expedition would be unsettling. To such a reader, what Calder Marshall said about the African equatorial forest and the traditional African imagination might be illuminating: "Whereas other peoples, inhabiting lands more domitable place the abodes of the dead either below the earth or in the sky the equatorial African can readily imagine the dead scouring deep within the jungle--" (*The Listener*, reprinted in *Critical Perspectives,* Lindfors, ed. 10). Emmanuel Obiechina reinforces this notion by saying that nature is not always conceived of as beneficent. In the traditional imagination, it is also full of threatening possibilities. The forest is full of mystery (*Culture, Tradition and Society in the West African Novel* 46). So, the drinkard, within the context or the setting that forged his existence is acting logically in making the bush and forest the home of the ageless enemy of mankind--death. As to the drinkard's fortification for this mythical undertaking, he has sublimated himself as the "Father of gods"; his juju and his father's juju--charms, give him added confidence. Having reinforced his human qualities of being empirical and rational with the metaphysical forces of magic and his mythical arrogation of being the "Father of gods," the drinkard is now duly qualified to grapple with "the physical, seen world and the unseen world of the gods, ancestors, spirits, witches" (Obiechina 38), and any other absurdities on his way to Deads Town.

When we hear from him again after seven months on his mythical adventure, he has already started to confront the usual riddle-solving tasks of "heroic myth". It is fitting that his first encounter would be with an old man who was "not a really man" but a god. This would validate the drinkard's claim of being the "Father of gods" and test the efficacy of his "juju".The drinkard holds his ground with this old man--god: they converse as equals, eat together and exchange wit as knowledgeable adversaries. The old man--god sends the drinkard on a menacing mission to capture death and bring him home in a big net. To the drinkard, this is not an impossible task. In the traditional folk-world that created him, all nature is humanized, and the intercourse between the living and the dead and spirit gods is possible (Obiechina, "Amos Tutuola and Oral Tradition," reprinted in Critical Perspectives). The drinkard does not only share cultural and physical proximity with Death, but he enjoys personal comradery with him--they converse as macho equals:

> After he [Death] was released by the ropes of yams and yam stakes, he came to his house and met me at his verandah, then we shook hands together, he told me to enter the house, he put me to one of his rooms, and after a while, he brought food to me and we ate it together, after that we started conversations which went thus:--He (Death) asked me from where did I come? I replied that I came from a certain town which was not so far from his place. Then he asked what did I come to do? I told him that I had been bearing about him in my town and all over the world and I thought within myself one day I should come and visit or to know him personally. After that he replied that his work was only to kill the people of the world, after he got up and told me to follow him and I did so. (13)

As could be seen, Death has met his equal in the drinkard. By implication, man's ageless preoccupation with the thought of containing death is exemplified by the drinkard's mythical encounter with Death in which he temporarily subdued death and made a public spectacle of him:

> When it was 6 O'clock in the morning, I went to his door and woke him up as usual, then told him that I wanted to return to my town this morning, so that I wanted him to lead me a short distance; then he got up from his bed and he began to lead me as I told him, but when he led me to the place that I had dug, I told him to sit down, so I myself sat down, on the road

> side, but as he sat down, on the net, he fell into the pit,
> and without any ado I rolled up the net with him and
> put him on my head and I kept going to the old man's
> house who told me to go and bring Death. (14-15)

As the old man--god would not be around to receive the trophy he had asked for, the drinkard has no other choice than to drop his curious load before the old man's door. The drinkard must now continue his adventure, having extinguished death from his consideration. However, in his new capacity as a mythical hero, he has assumed a fresh role of cultural interpreter of natural phenomena and events. The escaping of Death from the broken net must be given a cultural--universal significance. So, before he continues his quest for his dead tapster, the drinkard offers mythological explanation of why death is abroad in the world: "So that since that day that I had brought Death out from his house, he has no permanent place to dwell or stay, and we are hearing his name about in the world" (16).

After the drinkard's capture of Death and his consequent escape due to broken net, the drinkard has another assignment from a different agent--this time, the headman of a village he has entered after five months of his encounter with Death. The headman demands that the drinkard find his daughter who was enchanted and ensnared by "a curious creature from the market--, and bring her to him." Only then would the headman reveal the whereabouts of the tapster, the fateful--object of the drinkard's harrowing adventure through bushes and forests. The drinkard must not refuse this task; if he does, he would deflate the mythic import of his assumed name, the "Father of gods": "I was about to refuse to go and find out his daughter--, but when I remembered my name I was ashamed to refuse. So I agreed to find out his daughter" (17). Through the story of the headman's ensnared daughter, the drinkard imparts a cultural moral lesson:

> But the daughter--was a petty trader and was due to be
> married before she was taken away from the market.
> Before that time, her father was telling her to marry a
> man, but she did not listen to her father; when her
> father saw that she did not care to marry anybody, he

gave her to a man for him self, but this lady refused to
marry that man who was introduced to her by her
father. So that her father left her to herself. (17-18)

The young lady in this story is deliberately satirized for
contravening traditional expectation in her society--she refused to
marry whomsoever her father approved. This satire is on the lure of
money and mere appearance in the female sex of the author's society.
If a woman is as beautiful as an angel, and no man could convince her
for marriage, she has herself to blame, if "A Full-Bodied Gentleman
Reduced To Head" becomes her logical choice.

Culturally speaking, the headman's daughter, by her flagrant
refusal to marry her father's choice, has violated time-honored
tradition. Her being claimed by the demon--"the Skull as a Complete
Gentleman" should draw no tears in her community. But as the
drinkard in his new role as the "Father of gods" and mythical hero
must continue to have opportunity to perform his regenerative and
liberating feats, his sympathetic identification with this oppressed
lady is reasonably expected. The drinkard then on setting his eyes on
"The Skull As A Complete Gentleman," immediately absolved the
lady of any blame: "I could not blame the lady for following the Skull
as a complete gentleman to his house at all. Because if I were a lady,
no doubt I would follow him to wherever he would go,--" (25). The
drinkard with this excuse paves the way for his nightmarish encounter
with the Skull and his relatives--fellow skulls in their underground
demonic hole. Through his powers as the "Father of gods" and his
ritual fortifications as "a juju-man," he out-witted and over-powered
these mythical adversaries and freed the headman's daughter. The
drinkard has now acquired a wife and tells us so in his own words:
"This was how I got a wife." From what has transpired so far in the
story, the drinkard has consistently kept his actions within the
conventional expectations of his character-mode--the myth-hero of
literature. As we have seen, he is steadily confronting "the familiar
figures of heroic myth"--the task-masters who stipulate superhuman
chores to test his endurance, intelligence and wizardry-- characteristic
qualities of his Western counterparts (Odysseus, Aeneas, Jason and
others). In his recent feat of acquiring a wife as a result of his

exploits, the drinkard again satisfies what O. R. Dathorne describes as the "sine qua non of the myth-hero" (*African Literature in the Twentieth Century* 94). The reference here is, of course, to what Gerald Moore terms, "the ever-faithful and helpful female companion (Dante's Beatrice, Theseus' Adriadne, Jason's Medea)" (*Seven African Writers* 46).

From this point on to the end of the story (novel), the drinkard and his acquired wife are inseparable . Together, they endure indescribable punishment and humiliations from a precocious and horrible half-bodied baby that emanated from the swollen left thumb of the drinkard's wife. They must carry this prodigy of a child on their backs, day and night, and they must not eat anything because the child consumes everything in sight (32). This "Mog-bon juba", a figure in Yoruba folklore ("Child-Wiser-Than-His-Father") must be eliminated through appropriate rituals in order for the drinkard and his wife to continue their journey. As we learn from the drinkard himself, this is effected by "Three good creatures [who] took over our trouble--they were--Drum, Song and Dance" (38). It is logical that these three media, regarded in traditional African custom as consummate ritual-- spirits of placation and communal harmony should convey the appeasement.

The drinkard and his wife continue their journey after dispensing of their half-bodied baby. The going from this point becomes very treacherous for husband and wife. This gives the drinkard unbounded opportunities to continue to utilize his mythical calibres of being the "Father of gods," a strategist, juju-man who could out-trick and command compliance from his demonic adversaries. He invariably turns into "a big bird" (40), "a canoe" (39), "a pebble," "a lizard," for "the purpose of getting the better of his adversaries." For the drinkard and his wife, there is no going back now. They have decided to continue their journey to Deads' town even after they have received repeated warnings that no road leads to Deads' town, and that only the dead live there. Nothing would deter the drinkard from finding his dead palm-wine tapster. By this willingness at self-immolation, this readiness to die for a worthy cause (the drinkard's quest turned out to be such in the end), the drinkard continues to add to his stature as a mythical hero. An adventure that started as a selfish journey of appetite is steadily becoming an ennobling pilgrimage for the benefit of mankind in general. On their way to Deads' Town, the drinkard and his wife are subjected to various types of hardships: physical tortures, starvation, humiliations, from various malevolent monsters; they endure all without any self-pity. The drinkard's heroic experience with "The Red-People in The Red-Town" is indicative of his commitment to life and moral principle. He volunteers to die for the community of The Red-People, but in the end kills the Red-fish that exerted annual human sacrifice from them. This is a feat of mythical heroism. As we know, the didactic imperative in myth cautions "that man himself, by heroic action or sacrifice, must renew the energy of his world and keep it in equipoise" (Moore 51). As the drinkard fights his way to his eventual destination, Deads' Town, winning contest after contest, he finds time to make some cogent moral observation for the edification of man in general. His observation about the "unknown creatures" he and his wife encountered on their way to "Unreturnable Heaven's Town" presents a lesson to us: "These unknown creatures were doing everything incorrectly--the whole of them did not wash their bodies at all, but washed their animals (59). Metaphorically, "domestic animals," in the drinkard's observation symbolize human passions. The drinkard seems to be saying that when man drifts into moral darkness, human passions are keenly worshiped and given pride of place. At this juncture, we are heartened by the drinkard's moral insight--foreshadowing his total regeneration at the end.

        In "The Unreturnable Heaven's Town," the drinkard and his wife are severely tormented until they are rescued by an eagle: "When the eagle saw that they wanted to nail our heads, then it drove all of them away--" (62). The eagle could be seen as a symbol of social justice and it provides the drinkard another bout of temporary regeneration. After their liberation by the eagle, the drinkard comes to recognize the guiding "Hands of the "Faithful Mother in the White tree" (67-68). Here, the importance of the Earth Goddess in African literature cannot be over-emphasized. The mythological nature of trees is also documented in *Weep, Not Child* (Ngugi 46) and in Achebe's novels. The "Faithful Mother in the White Tree" proves true to her maternal role--food and drink abound, but the drinkard is learning a lesson in self-discipline. He must continue his journey to "Deads' Town" for a face-to-face encounter with his dead tapster in order to hasten his permanent regeneration; he must continue to learn. So, the drinkard and his wife continue their journey through the bush again.

Eventually, the drinkard and his wife are forty miles away from Deads' Town, according to the drinkard's calculation. However, they dare not make a tragic mistake of entering Death's Town during the day because they have not died. His wife offers the solution to this riddle: "but when my wife knew the secret, then she told me that we should stop and rest at night" (95) and enter the town at dawn. On reaching Deads' Town, the drinkard learns an important lesson–that no living person is allowed to enter the town; that it belongs to the dead, that the dead hate to see living people, and that they detest blood as a sign of life. Their escort (a dead agent) drags the drinkard and his wife out of Deads' Town and sends for the tapster to meet them on the outskirt of town. So, after a journey of ten harrowing years, the drinkard meets his dead tapster face to face, but the tapster could not go back home with him--death is a finality. We learn from the dead tapster, the cultural belief of the author's society about what happens after death. It is important for us to remember that we are not hearing from the tapster directly; the drinkard in his capacity as a mythical hero is interpreting events for our benefit: "He said that after he had died in my town, he went to a certain place, which anybody who just died must go to first, because a person who just died could not come here (Deads' Town) directly. He said that when he reached, he spent two years in training and after he had qualified as a full dead man, then he came to Deads' Town–" (99-100). Among the Igbos and the Yorubas there is a floating folk belief which speculates that to die is merely to change places here on earth. The dead just move to another country or region very far away from their former home and continue living. As long as nobody discovers them, they could continue to live undisturbed.

If the drinkard must achieve a permanent regeneration, he must not continue his quest for the dead tapster indefinitely. He must find him and bring home some life-saving insight, some boon for the common good. The drinkard gets a magic egg from his dead tapster and heads home-wards with his wife. Ritualistically, the egg, in traditional African context, is a symbol of mythological "Eldorado." The tapster affirms this view in his admonition to the drinkard. The reporting is by the drinkard: "He told me–that the use of the egg was to give me anything that I wanted in this world and if I wanted to use it, I must put it in a big bowl of water, then I would mention the name of anything that I wanted" (101).

At last, the drinkard returns home after defeating all tribulations along the way through his magic, juju and resourcefulness. But the test is not yet over for him. If his ten-year journey is to mean anything, he must confront man's problems in this world and thereby take his place among his counter parts: Odysseus, Aeneas, Odumodu and others. The drinkard does prove himself--his stature as a mythical hero is established. On his arrival home, as he tells us:

> there was a great (FAMINE) and it killed millions of
> old people and uncountable adults and children, even
> many parents were killing their children for food– etc.
> Every plant and tree and river dried away for lack of
> the rain, nothing for the people to eat. (118)

Immediately, the magic egg becomes handy; performing as the tapster directed, the drinkard miraculously feeds his community and put a temporary stop to hunger. Dathorne calls the magic egg the drinkard's "power of life and death over mankind (97). It should be added, however, that the drinkard's greatest contribution to his community in particular, and to mankind in general, lies in his being instrumental in resolving the seniority quarrel between Heaven and Earth--the cause of the famine:

> I called the rest of the old people who remained and
> told them how we could stop the famine--. We made
> a sacrifice of two fowls, 6 kolas, one bottle of palm
> oil, and 6 bitter kolas--. (124)

Through the drinkard's insight and direction, the sacrifice is carried "to Heaven in heaven" (124). The result is immediate--rain begins to fall regularly and famine is no longer an issue (124). By this bold stroke of leadership and moral insight, the drinkard has helped to restore cosmological balance in his society; he, therefore, deserves their gratitude and our appreciation.

The author of *The Palm-Wine Drinkard* himself, Amos Tutuola, also deserves our sincere commendation for being the first in his society, at lest in English, to seize and pin down for us in writing the myths and legends of a non-literate culture (Anthony West, *The New Yorker*, December 5, 1953: reprinted in *Critical Perspectives*, Lindfors ed: 17). His facility in the use of English he evolves for himself, to bring to us the cultural intelligence of his people (African in general, and Yoruba in particular) from the dim recesses of mythical past must not be minimized. Whether we choose to quibble with his credentials as a novelist (he only finished standard six), or condescensionally choose to be amused by his apparently "baby English;" *The Palm-Wine Drinkard*, his first book (1952) has continued to compel attention. It should be read with a sense of undisparaging inclinations, over-stretched imagination, and emulative commitment.

WORKS CITED

Achebe, Chinua. *Things Fall Apart*. New York: Astor-Honor, Inc., 1959.

Agbobiyi, Gladys. From *Nigeria Magazine*, March/May, 1968, reprinted in *Critical Perspectives on Amos Tutuola*, Lindfors, Bernth, ed. Washington, D.C.: Three continents Press, 1975.

Calder-Marshall. From *The Listener*, November 13, 1952. Reprinted in *Critical Perspectives*, 1975.

Collins, Harold R. "Founding a New National Literature: The

Ghost Novels of Amos Tutuola", reprinted in *Critical Perspectives,* 1975.

Dathorne, O. R. *African Literature in the Twentieth Century.* Minneapolis: University of Minnesota Press, 1975.

Moore, Gerald. *Seven African Writers.* London: Oxford University Press, 1962.

Obiechina, Emmanuel. *Culture, Tradition and Society in the West African Novel.* London: Cambridge University Press, 1975.

Obiechina, E. N. "Amos Tutuola and Oral Tradition",reprinted in *Critical Perspectives,* Lindfors, ed., 1975.

Ngugi, James. *Weep Not, Child.* New York: Collier Books, 1969.

West, Anthony. From *The New Yorker,* December 5, 1953. Reprinted in *Critical Perspectives,* Lindfors, ed., 1975.

Chapter Three

Superstition and the Riddle of Power in Achebe's *Arrow of God*

Arrow of God (1964) is the last of Achebe's culture contact trilogy novels. Our interest in this discussion is in Achebe's ambivalent treatment of the protagonist, Ezeulu--the Chief Priest of the Deity, Ulu, the protector of Umuaro clan. The author injects this ambivalence through the use of critical praise of Ezeulu. He is portrayed as the preserver of Umuaro tradition, yet his actions facilitate its dismantling; he is presented as a vessel of cultural uprightness, yet he is made to exude intransigent arrogance; he is said to be selfless, yet he acts and thinks as a self-serving, insensitive, vindictive person. This ambivalent portrayal of Ezeulu brews inconsistency, confusion, and defeat in this stalwart of a character, thereby, leaving the reader unsure as to where the author's sympathies lie in this history recreating fiction.

As the novel opens we see Ezeulu immersed in his role as the Chief Priest of Ulu. In this role he is both the sacerdotal functionary as well as keeper of the Umuaro seasonal calendar of farming events. At this juncture in the novel, he is preoccupied with his awesome responsibility of accurately espying and announcing the new moon to the six villages of Umuaro clan. By the ritual ordinance of his office, Ezeulu has to keep in his possession twelve "sacred yams", which he must consume one at a time following the appearance of each new moon. No harvest would ensue in Umuaro until he eats the twelfth yam corresponding with the Umuaro lunar year. This final act of the year heralds the day for the New Yam Festival. In this our initial encounter of Ezeulu, he has already eaten three of the sacred yams and is now in the process of eating the fourth, meaning that the festival of the Pumpkin Leaves is at hand. As he calculates the market date for this event and plans to send for his deputies to inform them to announce the day of the festival, we empathize with him as a faithful and caring upholder of Umuaro tradition--a solitary functionary of his deity and people.

After giving the reader such a beneficial and appealing profile of Ezeulu, Achebe seemed to have realized that awesome power and unbridled ego could easily corrupt a person especially, when that individual could not discriminate between invested and personal power. Ezeulu has this problem. Whether it is by design or by artistic confusion, the author then launches his protagonist into a maze of inconsistent behavior. The question here is whether Achebe through such portrayal is "cynical toward Ezeulu" as Dathorne asserts (73), or is this handling of Ezeulu a fictional accident. Whichever mold it fits, it is apparent that Achebe's treatment of his protagonist is full of ironies (Obiechina 174).

Let us examine some of these ironies--these inconsistencies and see how they cumulatively constitute a riddle of power in Ezeulu's fetish role as the Chief Priest of Ulu. As we have observed above, Ezeulu has difficulty distinguishing between invested and personal power. Achebe has used this weakness as a courier for his inconsistent characterization of the Chief Priest. Ezeulu's actions and response to people and events are heavily colored by this unfortunate trait. For example, after sending for his assistants in preparation for the announcement of the feast of the Pumpkin Leaves, he engages in a tragic contemplation on the nature of his power over Umuaro:

> Whenever Ezeulu considered the immensity of his power over the year and the crops and, therefore, over the people he wondered if it was real. It was true he named the day for the feast of the Pumpkin Leaves and the New Yam feast; but he did not choose the day. He was merely a watchman. His power was no more than the power of a child over a goat that was said to be his. As long as the goat was alive it was his; he would find it food and take care of it. But the day it was slaughtered he would know who the real owner was. (3)

Resenting the idea that he, Ezeulu is holding the fort for any other entity or entities, he continued his internal monologue thus: "No! The Chief Priest of Ulu was more than that, must be more than that. If he should refuse to name the day there would be no festival-- no planting and no reaping" (3).

In his tragic reverie Ezeulu has forgotten that his priestly office would cease the day he would refuse to announce the date of any of the two important festivals in the farming cycle of Umuaro clan. On second thought, however, he seems to have sensed the implication of his spurious nibbling at the time-honored custom and tradition of his office. He then equivocates: "But could he refuse? No Chief Priest had ever refused. So it could not be done. He would not dare." (3) In his portrayal as a vainglorious power monger, Ezeulu vehemently refuses the sobering, cautionary imperative of 'He would not dare.' He then gloats in his power by asserting that, "No man in all Umuaro can stand up and say that I dare not. The woman who will bear the man who will say it has not yet been born" (4). Even this scolding of an imaginary enemy could not assuage Ezeulu's incessant probing into the nature of his power; "What kind of power was it if everybody knew that it would not be used? Better to say that it was not there . . ." (4) As with Oedipus' tragic quest for the truth about King Laius' death, this speculative dilemma on the part of Ezeulu about the nature of his power is tragically foreboding. As we shall see later on in this discussion, it is Ezeulu's insistence of using his power . . . his invested power as personal toward the end of the novel that makes K. W. J. Post's observation in his "Introduction" to the 1969 edition of *Arrow of God* a disconcerting reality: "Ezeulu is a man of power and great pride in that power, yet his pride brings about the destruction of his power and that of the god he serves" (xi).

Of course, Ezeulu in his capacity as the Chief Priest of Ulu has power--invested ritual power to guide and preserve the tradition of Umuaro. This pride in his power, however, should neither be vaunted nor personal; it should emanate from a selfless feeling of satisfaction in priestly ordinance precisionally kept. Anyone who has read *Arrow of God* with impartial appreciation would agree that Ezeulu has reverential devotion to his office, but as events bear out in the novel it seems that Achebe has ironically introduced some tragic flashbacks to vitiate Ezeulu's role in the "preserving" aspect of that ordinance. In this instance, two flashbacks are remarkably worth discussing.

One of these jarring retrospection reminds the reader of the land feud between Umuaro and Okperi in which Ezeulu played a very controversial role to tip the balance in favor of Okperi, his mother's birth place before Mr. Winterbottom, the District Commissioner five years before the events of the novel commenced. It could be said that Ezeulu's problem with Umuaro clan started with this land dispute. Prior to their appearance before the white man whose colonization of Igbo land is now complete, Ezeulu has warned his clan that the land belonged to Okperi. He cautioned: "If you choose to fight a man for a piece of farmland that belongs to him I shall have no hand in it. He explains how he learned the truth about the land in dispute from his father (17). The question that needs to be asked here is: Is Ezeulu really impartial in his stand, or is he protecting his motherland? Achebe is equivocal here. Rather he juxtaposes the counter appeal of Nwaka, a titled powerful orator of Umuaro to Ezeulu's. Acknowledging the principle that a father does not tell a lie to his son, Nwaka insinuates that a father does not give what he does not have, any way. "Wisdom" he says, "is like a goatskin bag: everyman carries his own. Knowledge of the land is also like that." He emphasizes that his own father told him a different story about the land in question (17-18). In the belligerent role he is cast in this novel, Ezeulu pleads angrily and accusingly in vain to dissuade Umuaro from going to war with Okperi. He warns that Ulu would not support them. His pompous, omniscient stance and his perceived deference to his motherland moved the people of Umuaro to Nwaka's persuasion (20).

For days Umuaro and Okperi are locked in deadly war over land dispute and people are being killed on both sides. But the manner in which the war comes to an abrupt end indicates that a new dispensation has actually begun in Umuaro. As Achebe informs us in the novel, "The next day, . . . saw the war brought to a sudden end. The white man, Wintabota brought soldiers to Umuaro and stopped it. The story of what these soldiers did in Abame was still told with fear, and so Umuaro made no effort to resist but laid down their arms . . ." (31). In the judgement that ensued, the white man gave "the disputed land to Okperi" (31). This fateful outcome of the war and the land dispute gives Ezeulu an apparent misinterpretation of the whole incident. He sees it as a vindication of his stand and proof that his deity, Ulu is still very much in charge. What a bafflement! This perception of his deity in the face of the new realities in Umuaro (Colonial Administration and the Christian Mission are now firmly in control), will come back to haunt him in his final test of nerves with Umuaro clan later on in the novel. Emmanuel Obiechina, an Igbo scholar and critic summarizes Ezeulu's circumstance in this regard thus: "Ezeulu fails because his grasp of the situation is inadequate and so he is constantly surprised" (179). By implication, therefore, Achebe by consistently pulling the rug from off the Chief Priest's feet is insisting that the era of Abame slave raiders that gave life to Ulu and his priest is now an anachronism.

Another flashback that puts Ezeulu in a contradictory position of his role as the keeper and preserver of Umuaro tradition is the revelation that two years earlier he sent one of his sons to be part of the new religion. Ezeulu's advice to his son, Oduche as he sends him to join the new religion smacks of selfishness and ego-tripping. He explains his action thus: "I want one of my sons to join these people and be my eye there. If there is nothing in it you will come back. But

if there is something there you will bring home my share. The world
is like a mask dancing. If you want to see it well you do not stand in
one place. My spirit tells me that those who do not befriend the white
man today will be saying had we known tomorrow" (50-51). Ezeulu's
admonition to his son is fraught with ambiguities. Is it foresight? If
so, why would Ezeulu not respond to the white man's invitation to
Okperi Headquarters later on in the novel? If it is selfishness, as this
writer perceives it to be, why is Ezeulu portrayed as a selfless,
communal functionary? Why should he later blame Umuaro for
abandoning him to the white man? Why should he bring untold
hardship on Umuaro, the clan whose well-being is the reason for his
being by his refusal to announce the day for the New Yam Festival?
By these two actions--his testimony against his people before the
white man, and his sending Oduche to the Christian school, Ezeulu
has already two strikes against him before Umuaro people. And each
of these actions diminishes Ezeulu's credibility and thus his ritual
status among his people. Obiechina's observation on these effronteries
is worth noting here: "Taken together, the two events look like an
attempt by the Chief Priest to reach a personal accommodation with
the forces threatening the old social order. And this renders his
motives suspicious and dishonorable to his enemies and disturbing to
his friends" (176). This is very true. On the strength of these two
actions, Nwaka, Ezeulu's outspoken enemy sees him as "a man of
ambition; who wants to be king, priest, diviner, all" (30). His best
friend, Akuebue rebukes him for delving into the past to justify his
actions. He reminds Ezeulu that"what happened in [his father's and
his grandfather's] time and what is happening today are not the same;
[that his] father and grandfather did not do what they did to please a
stranger . . ." (150). So, Ezeulu presented to us earlier in *Arrow of
God* as a beacon of Umuaro tradition is now seen and perceived as a
leader of divided loyalties.

    Achebe in this novel is always confounding Ezeulu. The Chief
Priest by sending his son "to the new mission school to learn the
secret of the strangers" has hoped to acquire "added power"
(Dathorne 72). As with his lot in this tragic story, the fall out from
this apparently innocuous action is both devastating and baffling to
Ezeulu and the entire Umuaro clan. Ironically, the son that Ezeulu

sends to join the new religion is the same person who boxes and nearly suffocates the royal python--an emanation of the deity, Idemili, the patron of Umunnora, one of the villages of Umuaro. This incident is considered a taboo--a sacrilege. We may interpret it as unfortunate coincidence occasioned by ill conceived religious zeal on the part of Oduche, but the whole Umuaro has concluded that "Ekwensu's hand is in it"--the devil was responsible for this mishap. Privately and openly people accuse Ezeulu of a planned assault to undermine the authority of Ezeidemili whose friend Nwaka is Ezeulu's "mortal enemy." In the quarrel that ensues between Ezeulu, and his first son, Edogo, over Oduche's boxing of the royal python, we hear Edogo's hint at his father's ambivalence when he retorts to Ezeulu's rebuke that he, Edogo did not defend him before his detractors: "When you were my age your father did not send one of his sons to worship the white man's god" (58). Even Ezeulu's reception of the messenger from Ezeidemili to ascertain what the Chief Priest would do to purify his home of the abomination done there proves very combative. "Go back and tell Ezeidemili to eat shit . . . . Tell Ezeidemili that Ezeulu says he should go and fill his mouth with shit" . . . (59) This sort of errant behavior is unbecoming of a leader whose traditional role is to stay the course.

Finally, the Ezeulu we encounter in chapter seven as he re-enacts the ritual of the first Feast of the Pumpkin Leaves and carries the sins of all Umuaro to be buried before the shrine of Ulu, contrasts greatly with the Chief Priest presented to us later on in the novel. In this portrayal Ezeulu performs his function as a selfless servant of Ulu and public functionary of his people. Through him we learn that he recognizes and appreciates public support: "I carried my Alusi and, with all the people behind me, set on the journey. A man sang with the flute on my right and another replied on my left. From behind the heavy tread of all the people gave me strength" (81). This means that when Ezeulu submerges the mortal in him--his combative intuition, which makes an enemy of everyone who has a different opinion, he wins the people's support and their good-will.

We see this combative intuition at work as Ezeulu and Akuebue, his age-mate and best friend reason things out together following the aftermath of the royal python incident, and Ezeulu's two months' detention at the white man's Headquarters at Okperi. As a trusted friend Akuebue has come to confer with Ezeulu and to apprize him of public opinion in Umuaro over his perceived indiscretion in sending Oduche to the white man's school, thereby, indirectly precipitating the present desecration of the clan. The Chief Priest who has just recently edified his people about the efficacy of public support as he celebrates the Feast of the Pumpkin Leaves, now reveals himself to be insensitive to public opinion. He asserts before his friend: "I know that Umuaro is divided and confused and I know that some people are holding secret meeting to persuade others that I am the cause of the trouble. But why should that remove sleep from my eye . . . We are still waiting, Ulu and I, for that beast to come and unseat us . . ." (147) The "beast", of course, refers to Nwaka, the titled aristocrat who sees Ezeulu as a man of ambition, who is steadily arrogating to himself the trappings of a king. In his continued vendetta Ezeulu asks some presumptuous questions: "Who tells the clan what it say? What does the clan know? (147)

From the above utterances, it is apparent that Ezeulu is seeing himself and Ulu as one and the same entity and has forgotten how the six villages of Umuaro created the Deity out of expediency. As he continues to wallow in self justification, his friend emphatically delivers to him the consensus of the people in these terms: "But you forgot one thing: that no man however great can win judgement against a clan. You may think you did in that land dispute but you are wrong. Umuaro will always say that you betrayed them before the white man. And they will say that you are betraying them again to day by sending your son to join in desecrating the land"(148). Akuebue's words are readily vindicated. Ezeulu is about to experience the greatest and untested riddle of his sacerdotal office. His friendship with the white man has come full circle to haunt him. In Okperi where the vogue of colonial system of Indirect Rule is putting pressure on the District Commissioner to appoint a Warrant Chief for Umuaro, Mr. Winterbottom has already sent some messengers to bring Ezeulu to him for a "preliminary discussion." He intends to confer the honor of a warrant chief on his friend who has the audacity to testify against his people in the land dispute and allow his son to join the white man's religion.

In the tragic confusion that ensues due to incompatible protocols--Ezeulu's and the white man's, the Chief Priest could not honor Mr. Winterbottom's invitation promptly. Rather, he calls a meeting of Umuaro to seek their opinion and support in this dilemma. The Umuaro deny Ezeulu their support but strongly volunteer their opinion. They advise him to go to Okperi to visit his friend, the white man and that it is customary for friends to visit friends. Meanwhile, Mr. Winterbottom on learning of Ezeulu's response orders that he be detained on his arrival. For two months Ezeulu is detained in Okperi Headquarters and could not eat the rest of his ritual yams and thus, announce the Feast of the New Yam. Is Ezeulu worried about this interruption? Is he mindful of the starvation that would devastate Umuaro because no family could harvest its yams before the New Yam Festival? As he reflects on his detention, Ezeulu relishes this interruption because it would enable him to settle old scores with his people (181). On his return, he continues to hold out; not even the delegation of titled elders would persuade him to call the New Yam Festival and thus relieve Umuaro from starvation. This is sheer vindictiveness. In his zest for revenge Ezeulu loses sight of his clan's symbiotic and pragmatic relationship with their gods. He forgets that there was a time Ulu, his deity was not in existence, and that Umuaro who installed it has the collective option of dislodging both deity and priest should they prove intransigent.

This is what happens to Ulu and his priest, though, symbolically. To arrest starvation in Umuaro, the head of the new religion announces that whoever makes his thanks offering to God could harvest his crops without fear of Ulu (246). As Achebe tells us at the last page of the novel,". . . many an Umuaro man had sent his son with a yam or two to offer the new religion and bring back the promised immunity. Thereafter any yam that was harvested in the man's fields was harvested in the name of the son" (262). It seems that Ezeulu has put himself and his deity out of business by his intransigent refusal in the words of David Carroll, "to abrogate one iota of the authority invested in Ulu and by extension in himself . . . ." (100). What Ezeulu forgets is that Ulu is not to blame in whatever happens in this story. After all, it is a mere creation of the people to forge a united front against a menacing evil--specifically, the Abame slave raiders of the early and mid-nineteenth century.

Now that the new century--the twentieth, with its new realities, (the colonial administration and its Christian institutions, has made such a threat irrelevant), Ezeulu should have used extreme caution in testing the nature of his power over Umuaro. But he fails to understand that the superstitious mores that nourished his power in the past are now on the wane. Perhaps, Ezeulu needs to be portrayed in the manner he is depicted by Achebe in *Arrow of God* as a warning that those who would protect some moribund tradition and custom with unyielding zest risk being the sacrificial victims of the new.

Works Cited

Achebe, Chinua. *Arrow of God.* New York: Doubleday and Company, Inc., 1969.

Carroll, David. *Chinua Achebe*. New York: Twayne Publishers, Inc. 1970.

Dathorne, O.R. *African Literature in the Twentieth Century.* Minneapolis: University of Minnesota Press, 1975.

Obiechina, Emmanuel. "the Human Dimension of History in *Arrow of God,*" *Critical Perspectives on Achebe*. Ed. C. L. Innes and Bernth Lindfors. Washington, D.C.: The Three Continents Press, (1978): 170-179.

Chapter Four

John Grimes as Metaphor in
Go Tell It on the Mountain

Introducing the chapter entitled, "Selected Writings" reprinted in his book, *James Baldwin: The Legacy*, Quincy Troupe puts an insert of Baldwin's words on the role of the writer and his affinity to the truth in these terms: "Truth is a two-edged sword--and if one is not willing to be pierced by that sword, even to the extreme of dying on it, then all of one's intellectual activity is a . . . delusion and a wicked and dangerous fraud" (219). This means that the writer--the writer of fiction, for that matter--must embrace the imaginative exploration of life, for this is what fiction is, with a bold and unequivocal commitment to authorial veracity. Writers of this caliber spare no one, not even themselves, their ethnic groups or even their country--in their abrasive and unrelenting depiction of life and living. To discharge this onerous responsibility, writers of fiction create their different platforms as vantage points from which they observe, assay and promulgate their diagnosis of society's moral

health for the benefit of man. In *Go Tell It on the Mountain* Baldwin
portrays John as a metaphor of resilience, and in the process of
finding salvation John becomes the platform from which the author
examines, exposes, and excoriates religious hypocrisy and,
inferentially, the state of the African American family and the social
and economic disenfranchisement of African Americans.

As laid out above, Baldwin's portrayal of John in *Go Tell It on
the Mountain* is metaphorical, a multidimensional portrayal lending
itself to diverse contextual sympathies. To foster this design, the
author makes John part of the "Harlem Holy Rollers" (Vinslow 637-
38)--"three generations of the Grimes--[who are emotionally in]
search for Jesus with focus on the storefront Church as a transition
between the rural life of their ancestral South and the alien tenement
of the North" (Ottley 7). On the morning of his fourteenth birthday,
John, the partial narrator and participant in a story of which he is the
protagonist, becomes increasingly aware of his surroundings. As we
follow this precocious child's life experience in a family where he
tries in vain to fathom the cause of his father's lovelessness towards
him (though we know the reason--he was born out of wedlock) as he
struggles in bewilderment to grapple with the disparate condition of
his people in a society where the opulence of Fifth Avenue was
forbidden to Negroes, as he silently sheds tears over "the deep frown
in [his mother's] forehead", as he wonders aloud about the wisdom of
"the Way of the Cross," and as he mutely despises the God that has
treated him and his people unfairly, Baldwin's subtle use of language
corrals our imagination and excites our interest in John's religious
odyssey in this novel.

In his indictment of organized religion, Baldwin uses the
Christian Cross as "a dubious icnographic symbol" threatening to
destroy the very life it ostensibly nurtures and protects" (Porter 102).
This observation is vindicated in *Go Tell It on the Mountain* in the
person of Gabriel and his menacing use of the Church for his own
selfish and diabolical designs. At this juncture, Horace Porter's
characterization of Baldwin's narrative technique of focusing on
relationships is relevantly functional in this discussion of *Go Tell It
on the Mountain*. With this narrative paradigm, John is presented to
us in the first section of the book in relation to the Reverend Gabriel

Grimes, the only father he knows--his stepfather. According to Porter, Baldwin by this technique "lets us know that a principal theme of [this novel) will be paternal priority--the inescapable consequences of a father's life working themselves out in the life of a son" (114-115). Porter quotes the opening sentence of the novel to underscore this assertion: "Everyone had always said that John sees and hears what he hears about Gabriel Grimes, his stepfather, at home and in "The Temple of the Fire Baptized" (115).

From this information Baldwin gives us a double-barreled perspective on religious hypocrisy and the state of the African-American family. We see Gabriel, God's anointed holy deacon, in his home where he is the head and presumed shepherd of his flock. But before our encounter with him in the late afternoon of John's fourteenth birthday, we, like John, cannot understand the secret import of Elisabeth's admonition to her son in these words: "I . . . know there's a whole lot of things you don't understand. But don't you fret. The Lord'll show you in His own good time everything He wants you to know. You put your faith in your Lord, and He'll surely bring you out . . . Everything works together for good for them that love the Lord" (24). John's response to this motherly talk after some ponderous observation of his mother's silent agony in his father's household is "Yes Mama, I'm going to try to love the Lord" (25). We shall return to this secret pact between mother and son later in this discussion. In the meantime, let us return to the present scene and follow John home from his birthday outing made possible by the money his mother gave him before pronouncing her baffling admonition. Using Roy's stab-wound, his father's reaction to this circumstance and Gabriel's audacity in bad-mouthing and manhandling his wife, Elizabeth, and reviling John, his step-son, Baldwin gives the reader a foreboding picture of a loveless and tenuous family unit: "Father and Mother knelt by the sofa where Roy lay . . . . Father was washing the blood from Roy's forehead, muttering sweet, frenzied things to Roy. Mother's touch would have been more gentle, but Father thrust her aside. He could not bear to have anyone else touch his wounded son" (31-32).

Now addressing John, Gabriel asks, "Where you been, boy, all this time? . . . Don't you know you's needed here at home" (32)?

These two questions in normal family circumstances would have been readily in order, but Gabriel's perverse and diabolical attitude toward John and his mother, Elizabeth, could not escape John 's intuition: "More than his words, Father's face caused John to stiffen with fear and dislike. There was more than anger in Father's face . . . In the moment that his father's eyes swept over him, John knew that his father hated him because he was not on the sofa instead of Roy" (32-33). Later, as we learn from Gabriel's flashback on the early years of his marriage to Elizabeth, we recoil and ask what gives Gabriel the moral gut to taunt Elizabeth who begot John out of wedlock. Responding to Gabriel's question if she had truly repented of her sins, Elizabeth lashes out:

> "I know you ain't asking me to say I'm sorry I brought Johnny into the world. Is you?" When Gabriel did not answer, Elizabeth added: "And listen, Gabriel I ain't going to let you make me sorry. Not you, nor nothing, nor nobody in the world. You and me is got two children, Johnny and Roy. And soon we's going to have three. I ain't going to make no difference amongst them. And you ain't going to make none either." (84)

We now know why Gabriel is angry with John for not being the victim of Roy's wound. The fine print of Gabriel's disposition toward John is further amplified by Louis Pratt, "When Elizabeth gave birth to Roy, Gabriel prayed that he might one day follow in his father's footsteps in the Church, but Roy had inherited his father's waywardness, and had no designs on the ministry whatsoever" (55).

Here, we see that John, Elizabeth and even Roy suffer and bear the brunt of Gabriel's past sins and psychological guilt, lending credence to Wole Soyinka's observation about Baldwin's singular artistry of seeing "the oppressor as also the oppressed" (17). Enlightened by this insight, we can confidently go to Gabriel's acidic taunting remarks about Elizabeth's inability to take adequate care of Roy and understand why her sharp retort unleashed Gabriel's hell fire on her. Elizabeth retorts, "You don't know what to do with this boy, and that's why you all the time trying to fix the blame on somebody. Ain't nobody to blame, Gabriel. You just better pray to God to stop Roy before somebody puts another knife in him and puts him in his grave" (38). The last sentence of Elizabeth's fateful observation above serves as a retrospective premonition in Gabriel's psychic reflex, which instantaneously flashes the picture of the manner of his first son's death before him. That son's name was Royal--the son he had with Esther while he was still married to Deborah, his first wife and was a deacon in the church. The unrecognized son of Gabriel died of a knife wound to his throat in Chicago (108-109). The Roy now being treated for a stab-wound in Gabriel's Harlem apartment is named after the "royal son" of Gabriel's sinful past.

No wonder Elizabeth's apparently innocuous warning about what could be the logical conclusion of Roy's life, if his rascality continues, ignites an emotional firestorm in Gabriel. John, the narrator of *Go Tell It on the Mountain* captures the bristling consequence by stating, "Mother and Father stared at each other, she with a startled, pleading question in her eyes. Suddenly Father reached out and, with all his might, slapped her across the face. She crumpled at once, hiding her face with one thin hand. Aunt Florence moved to hold her up, while Sarah watched with greedy eyes" (38-39). In the above scene, Baldwin seems to be emphasizing that this type of open scandal and gutless violation of the female partner of the marriage by the man, who professes to love and care for her, is an effrontery that is fraught with serious repercussions, especially, when it happens in front of her children. Yes, Sarah "watched with greedy eyes," but the more vocal and "headstrong" Roy could not tolerate such an insult on his mother lying down. His acrimonious protest against his father's banal act represents every child's resentment in like circumstance: "Don't you slap my mother. That's my mother. You slap her again, you black nigger, and I swear to God I'll kill you" (39)! For this provoked threat, Gabriel thrashes Roy mercilessly with his belt whispering, "My Lord," "my Lord," "my Lord." This exclamation implies that this beating is sanctioned by Gabriel's personal God, and John witnesses it all and sees his mother crying as he "had never seen a woman, or anybody cry before" (40).

With this type of behavior on the part of a man of God, an

ordained minister for that matter, and in a home supposed to have
been blessed by the sanctifying grace of matrimony, is it any wonder
that it would take John his fourteenth birthday to begin to consider
embracing his father's God in order to save his soul? It is interesting
that in this venture and in the face of his father's religious hypocrisy,
it would take the promptings of a teenage outsider to start John on his
way to finding salvation in this particular Saturday-night Tarry
Service of his fourteenth birthday: "Boy, ain't it about time you was
thinking about your soul? Don't you want to be saved, Johnny? Ain't
you just a-struggling and wanting the help of Jesus" (44)? Even with
Elisha's promptings, John cannot unburden his heart of the
contradictions of his father's house: his father's searing hatred of him
and his corresponding hatred of his father; the encroaching poverty of
his home, as symbolized by the unremitting dust and dirt of the
kitchen and living room; and the suggestive nihilism of his father,
which ascribes sin and damnation to every experience--all these
considerations tangle in John's mind as he experiences salvation's
initial throbbing in "The Temple of Fire Baptized" (44). He sees no
reason to clap and rejoice with the saints. "His heart told him he had
no right to sing or to rejoice" (47).

But we, the readers who identify with him in his predicament
in his father's house and who know of Gabriel's many sins and false
religiosity, want John to brave his circumstance and accept salvation
as our spite against Gabriel for his phoniness and his doctrine of non-
inclusive love. Baldwin's meticulous use of descriptive details to
document Gabriel's rendezvous with sins of infidelity and religious
hypocrisy sharpens our disgust for Gabriel for "not using his
privileged position of love and opportunity," as Trudier Harris puts
it, "as wisely as he should" (26-27). Specifically, we learn from these
flashbacks how Gabriel exploited Deborah, a rape victim by inviting
her to church and telling her "that the Lord had led him to ask her to
be his wife" (81). We also learn of his double perfidy against her later
by his affair with Esther, a girl he also invites to Church and steals
Deborah's savings to send her away on his learning of her pregnancy.
We further learn of his scandalizing and heartless non-
acknowledgment of his son by Esther--his promised "royal son"
whose conception and birth belie Gabriel's claim to holiness (92-97),

and of Esther's scorching indictment of Gabriel in a letter ironically passed on to Gabriel by his all-seeing wife Deborah:

> What I think is, I made a mistake. That's true, and I'm praying for it now, but don't you think you ain't going to pay for it. I don't know when and I don't know how, but I know you going to be brought low one of these fine days. I ain't holy like you are, but I know right from wrong. I'm going to have my baby and I'm going to bring him up to be a man. And I ain't going to read to him out of no Bibles and I ain't going to take him to hear no preaching. If he don't do nothing but sit around and drink moonshine all his natural days, he still be a better man than his daddy. (97-98)

Unfortunately, Esther does not live to rear her child. Still from these flashbacks, we are also apprized of how Gabriel meets Elizabeth, his second wife and mother of John, and how he, with his usual ensnaring design, invites her to church and later reveals to her, "Sister Elizabeth . . . the Lord's been speaking to my heart. And I believe it's His will that you and me should be man and wife . . . And I'll love you. I'll honor you. . .until the day God calls me home . . . And I'll love your son, your little boy . . . just like he was my own . . ." (151-152). By this time we know better.

As we learn of these respective revelations about Gabriel and his diabolical past, we are reminded of John, as he lies on the threshing floor of the "Temple of the Fire Baptized," struggling and fighting with the doubting dilemma imposed upon his young but precocious mind by Gabriel's loveless and obstructionist disposition toward him. When John finally comes through, triumphantly satisfying what Saint Paul regarded as the sinequanon of Christian salvation--confession, John "whispered aloud in the Church, 'Oh, Lord, have mercy on me. Have mercy on me Lord'" (167). We are happily relieved by the realization that the table has now turned against Gabriel, and as Pratt has relevantly observed, "it is Gabriel himself who is desperately in need of redemption; he stands in need of deliverance from himself" (54). Even after his son has embraced his religion, his God to win his acceptance, Gabriel remains unbudged in his hatred of John. Emboldened by his new-found salvation, John stands before Gabriel and smiles a forgiving smile and utters, "Praise the Lord," a Christian greeting of love to his father, but Gabriel responds reluctantly in the same garb and "did not move to touch John, did not kiss him, did not smile" (Baldwin 174). In this instance, John realizes that his salvation is a matter between him and his God, notwithstanding the many indignities he has endured from his father; his courage and forbearance toward Gabriel, in spite of the latter's immovable hatred for him, make John a metaphor of resilience and inspiration for the oppressed and abused and bewildered by the cruel environmental predicaments beyond their knowledge and control.

Incredibly, it is the marvel of this writer how Baldwin, in keeping with the common sense admonition of Henry James to young writers of fiction, that all life, all human experience belongs to them, could masterfully execute a literary coup in *Go Tell It on the Mountain* to give us an honest reflection of his society. Whether we read and reflect on the circumstance that has robbed John of his natural father, Richard, and disposes his mother, Elizabeth, to be hitched to a wrong horse in Gabriel; whether we feel indignant at the racial gang rape which has made Deborah a victim of double perfidy in Gabriel's hand; whether we shudder with disbelief at the manipulative instinctive copulation by a religious con man, which sends Esther, a budding young black woman, to an early grave and leaves her son with Gabriel unclaimed and uncared for, we see each horror being played out for us in real life in the American social polity.

We are heartened that James Baldwin has given us John Grimes as an icon of indomitable spirit, to inspire our young-- especially our young black males to defy their odds by choosing life instead of self-immolation. For these young men to do so, we must be mindful, as Baldwin has inferentially instructed us, in the mentoring relationship between brother Elisha and John that they need some nurturing male presence to see them through.

Works Cited

Baldwin, James. *Go Tell It on the Mountain*. New York: A Falcon Book Edition-Noble and Noble, Publishers, Inc, 1968.

----, (An Insert) reprinted Quincy Troupe, Ed. *James Baldwin: The Legacy*. New York; Simon & Schuster, Inc, 1989.

Harris, Trudier. *Black Women in the Fiction of James Baldwin*. Knoxville: The University of Tennessee Press, 1985.

Porter, Horace. *Stealing the Fire: The Art and Protest of James Baldwin*. Middletown, Connecticut Wesleyan University Press, 1989.

Pratt, Louis H. *James Baldwin*. Boston: G. K. Hall & Company, 1978.

Ottley, Roi. "The Negro Seeks a Way Out." *Chicago Sunday Tribune Magazine of Books*. 12 July 1953:7.

Soyinka, Wole. "Forward: James Baldwin at the Welcome Table." *James Baldwin: The Legacy*. ed. Quincy Troupe. New York: Simon & Schuster, Inc., 1989.

Vinslow, Henry F. "Church Sermon." *The Crisis* 60 (December 1955): 637-33.

Chapter Five

Land, History and the Individual in *Weep not, Child*

Land, history and the individual serve as the three dimensional dynamics that converge to produce the intractable conflict in *Weep Not, Child* (1964), a first novel by Ngugi wa Thiong'o, (James Ngugi) a well known Kenyan novelist. The individual caught in this conflict is Njoroge, the child-protagonist, whose naive and idealistic perception of his role in restoring his people's stolen ancestral land through formal education, is shatteringly belied by pre-independence Kenyan history and politics reflected in the novel. Njoroge's attitude and ordeal in grappling with, or rather, reacting to the other two polemics of the novel, therefore, constitute the focal interest of this article.

In a radio interview with Dennis Duerden in England, 1972, six years after the publication of *Weep Not, Child,* Ngugi was asked about his acute interest in the land as revealed in his first published novel. His answer to this question underscores the all-embracing importance of the land to the Kenyan people: "It is more than the material; it is not just because of its economic possibilities; it is something almost akin to spiritual" (123). Anyone who has even had a cursory reading of *Weep Not, Child* will not have any difficulty in appreciating the consuming presence of the land in the novel. It is a way of life, a religion not to be violated without consequences. This inviolability of the land in the Kenyan psychic and culture is vividly and emotionally articulated in the story Njoroge's father Ngotho, told him and other Gikuyu boys and girls about the origin and sanctity of the land. The telling of the story is not accidental or frivolous. It is intended to imbue in the children a sacred and lasting knowledge of the contractual nature of the Gikuyu's custodianship of the land before colonial intrusion and meddling in Kenyan affairs.

According to this awesome mythology, the Creator, Murungu, created a very large expanse of land, not to be fathomed by any human eyes. On this land, God caused a holly tree to sprout and grow taller and taller. Then Murungu (God) created one man--Gikuyu and one woman, Mumbi and placed them under this holy tree with the injunction: "This land I hand over to you, O Man and Woman. It's yours to rule and till in serenity sacrificing only to me Your God, under my sacred tree" (*Weep Not, Child* 46). At this juncture, Njoroge could not contain his amazement at what happened to the land God had given to his ancestors. In his childish insensitivity to his father's pain over the loss of the land Njoroge asked the dreaded question: "Where did the land go?" (47). It is through his father's response to this curiosity that Njoroge learns of his people's involvement in the first World War, and the death of his only maternal brother in this war, and the displacement of his ancestors by colonial settlers. He also learns from his father's story that the land now owned by Mr. Howlands, a British settler, belonged to his ancestors (48). Worst of all, Njoroge learns to his dismay, that his father is compelled to work as a share cropper on the land that normally would belong to him.

Through the above story of what happened to land, Ngugi is making use of a very powerful historical allusion to chastise British colonial behavior in Kenya during the turn of this century. Specifically, the historical event in question here is "The British

Imperial Land Act of 1915 [which] transferred official ownership of all land to the British crown, giving the governor authority for its disposal . . . ." According to Cook and Okenimkpe, this power was "widely exploited . . . so that most Gikuyu were left without any legal rights over the soil of their homeland" (1). This historical colonial high-handedness made subsequent generations of Kenyan children, including the Njoroges and the Ngugis, to be born as disappropriated citizens in their country.

The cultural, emotional and political dissonance created among the Kenyan natives over several generations, as to the best means of retrieving the land from the usurpers, reached its highest pitch, during the childhood and adolescent years of Njoroge, the fateful protagonist of *Weep Not, Child*. In order to give a chronological context to Njoroge's two stages of development mentioned above, it is appropriate that *we* look at Ngugi's parallel development. Commenting on his schooling Ngugi revealed that he "first went to school in 1946 or '47 . . ." (125), and Gerald Moore maintains that Ngugi's school days at Kikuyu High School coincided with the Mau Mau war of Resistance which raged in the vicinity from 1952-1958" (262). It is to be said here that both the Mau Mau Resistance Movement and Ngugi's schooling were all considered effective instruments of retrieving the land as political independence, was in the words of Eustace Palmer, "synonymous with the repossession of the land" (1). The only difference in these two instruments lies in their respective approach, their pace of achieving the desired goal. The Mau Mau approach is physical, aggressive, impatient and intolerant of opposition or traitors. On the other hand, schooling (formal education) is slow and mainly contemplative in its agenda.

It is between these two polemics that the Ngugis—Njoroges of pre-independence Kenya must make the hard choices--either to stand up and be counted among the Mau Maus or to shun or delay involvement by finding solace in the contemplative copout of formal education. Given Njoroge's age, as ascertained from his author's parallel development at this particular period in Kenya's contemporary history, the spilling of blood, his and others, to repossess the land, would be extremely repugnant and overwhelming.

After all, he would be only twelve years of age by 1958, when the Mau Mau Resistance Movement reached its zenith.

This does not mean that the young Njoroge is uncaring or unaware of the central issue involved in the current conflict. He knows about the loss of the land; his father's story (46-49) has galvanized his imagination and sent him adreaming. His conversation with his friend, the daughter of Jacobo, as they pass through Mr. Howlands' estate reveals Njoroge's awareness. As they survey and admire the greenness and expanse of Mr. Howlands' farm, Njoroge instructs his friend, "All this land belongs to black people." Then Mwihaki rejoins, "Ye-e-s. I've heard Father say so. He says that if people had education, the white man would not have taken all the land. I wonder why our old folk, the dead old folk, had no learning when the white man came?" To this question, Njoroge responds: "There was nobody to teach them English." Mwihaki tells him that her father learned how to speak English "in the mission place . . . Siriana." (62)

For Njoroge, this incidental lesson on the value of formal education from Mwihaki is reinforced on all sides. He receives a frontal admonition from his beloved half brother, Kamau on the intrinsic value of the land and the necessity of formal education to combat its loss. Responding to Njoroge's incessant inquiry into why his half-brother is not going to school, Kamau reminds him of the poverty of their home because of their father's landlessness and that he, Kamau, is learning to be a carpenter so that he could help defray Njoroge's school expenses. He then delivers this reinforcing advice to Njoroge. "Your learning is for all of us. Father says the same thing. He is anxious that you go on, so you might bring light to our home. Education is the light of Kenya. That's what Jamo says" (63). Njoroge would later on hear this type of talk directly from his father, Ngotho. As they are all together at home one evening, his father proudly asks when his school would open. On being told when, Ngotho directs the following advice to Njoroge: "Education is everything . . . You must learn to escape the conditions under which we live. It is a hard way. It is not much that a man can do with out a piece of land" (64). For Njoroge, his father's advice is an imperative. He has listened and instinctively imbibed the "indefinable demand (being) made on him" in his young age (64).

He also remembers his mother's unspoken intention when she sends him to school the first time with this rhetorical injunction; "You won't bring shame to me by one day refusing to attend school?" (21). Nyokabi later on in her internal monologue reveals to us the real missionary intent of her sending her son to school. As a woman with an introspective and analytical insight, she could imagine the liberating benefits of formal education. She then thinks aloud: "If Njoroge could now get all the white man's learning, would Ngotho even work for Howlands and especially as the wife was reputed to be a hard woman? Again, would they as a family continue living as Ahoi (sharecroppers) in another man's land, a man who clearly resented their stay?" (37)

Hedged supportively on all sides by his family and the Gikuyu community and incessantly urged to continue to do well in school, Njoroge is unwittingly thrust into a messianic role in which he sees himself as the Moses of his people (65 & 137). From this ivory tower of childish fancies and bloated imagination, our hero would find euphoric security and solace within the sanitized confines of his mission schools. Yet, around Njoroge, the things he values very much are crashing, left and right. The union strike on which his people have pinned their hopes for decent wages and better treatment by their employers--the European settlers, has failed because of his father's aborted heroism (90). In retaliation for his role in the strike, his father Ngotho with his family is sacked from his homestead on Jacobo's land. Before Njoroge's eyes, his whole family is steadily disintegrating through the vicious collaboration of Mr. Howlands, a European settler turned farmer and eventually, District Officer with the obnoxious Jacobo, a native stooge, made Chief for his treacherous role against his people. The arrest of the legendary Jomo and his subsequent imprisonment has devastated the Ngotho family (110-11). These indignities and others help to galvanize the young men on the side of the Mau-Mau and make its membership a matter of patriotism.

In all of these happenings, Njoroge is still buoyant in his idealism, "Through all this, Njoroge was still sustained by his love for and belief in education and his own role when the time came . . . he actually saw himself as a possible savior of the whole God's country. Just let him get learning" (120). It is with this type of sentiment that Njoroge follows Mwihaki, his girl friend home to see and be seen by her father, a man who is methodically and vindictively working for the destruction of his father and his family. This brand of open-mindedness on the part of Njoroge is either foolhardy or nihilistic ignorance. Even Mwihaki the more realistic of the two friends, is fearful of her gun-wielding father for what he might have done.

She explains her fear to Njoroge, "I hate to think that he may have killed some man because at night he wakes and says that he heard some people talking of his own death. And people you know are always avoiding me, even girls of my age . . ." (13). In her desperation, she entreats her friend to elope with her, but Njoroge would not have that because it would ruin God's plan for him, "And what would God think of him if he deserted his mission like that?" (137).

But Njoroge's cocoon would burst with time and events. He would watch his beloved and revered Bible teacher, Isaka and other Christians massacred in cold blood by the soldiers of the Homeguard on the pretext that they were members of the Mau Mau Movement. Only a school identification card saves Njoroge from harm from the soldiers, at least for now. In the interim, his life continues to be, taunted by contradictions. Now he is jubilant over his remarkable success in his qualifying examination for high school. His two mothers, Nyokabi and Njeri are also happy for him, and even his famished father bedridden from the beatings and tortures he received from Mr. Howlands' homeguards could be seen all smiles at this "good news." Kamau, the only brother now at home is very supportive (147). Njoroge could perceive that his home was no longer the same.

However, in fairness to Njoroge, his unflinching interest in school is buttressed by his Gikuyu community of all persuasions. As has been reiterated in this paper and in *Weep Not, Child* itself, the Gikuyu people regard education as their means of political emancipation--of retrieving the land. Now that Njoroge has crossed the threshold in his education and is about to attend Siriana Secondary School, "a well-known center of learning" (151), he is "no

longer the son of Ngotho but the son of the land" [hence], many
people contributed money so that he could go" (148). There is nothing
wrong with this support on the part of the Gikuyu community, but it
does not excuse Njoroge from engaging in sober considerations. At
Siriana, he continues to dream and push the cringing realities of his
home from his consciousness. He wishes the whole country could be
like Siriana, enjoying peace and "Christian progress" (151-159).

At last, for our hero, the tenuous security of his home which
has insulated him from harm for the past nineteen years or
"thereabouts" (160), is dealt a final blow by Mr. Howlands and the
Homeguards at the murder of Chief Jacobo. In the rabid investigation
that follows the Chief's death Ngotho and his two wives Nyokabi and
Njeri are detained and mercilessly tortured at the Homeguards Post,
and Kamau, Njoroge's only brother still remaining at home, is
arrested and taken away. Even Njoroge, himself, would not be
allowed to complete his second year at Siriana. He is recalled to the
Homeguard Post and brutally tortured, until be goes into a coma and
wakes up, only to face more excruciating torture that nearly cost him
his manhood. He witnesses his castrated father die before him,
making him the sole keeper of the two women. Would he keep the
fort in memory of his father and his brothers who fought bravely for
what was theirs--the land? Would what he suffered in person at the
Post spur him into righteous indignation to fight like a man for what
is his--though "pressed to the wall, dying, but fighting back"?. Not at
all! Njoroge is still on the run and would have escaped to Uganda
with Mwihaki had not this level-headed young lady reminded him
that they were no longer children. With this apparent rebuff, and with
the circumstances of his home hanging over his neck, Njoroge
decides to take his own life and thereby escape his responsibilities
forever. However, through a last minute after-thought, Ngugi
ingenuously saves his hero from self-immolation through the guiding
voice of Nyakobi, the mother whose love and self-denial made it
possible for her son Njoroge to go to school in the first place.

At this point, Njoroge's emphatic response to his mother's call,
"Mother . . ." "I am here" (184) is indeed reassuring. His going home
with the two women his father left in his care and opening the door
for them is a final redeeming act of his accepting responsibility for

the first time in his life. From this glimmer of hope, we may have every reason to believe that the Njoroges of Kenya have done an invaluable service to their country's cause by choosing to stay alive, after all. The story of what happened to their people in their fierce but legitimate battle to retrieve the land must be told. As Achebe has emphasized in his recent novel, *Anthills of the Savannah*, "the battle drum is important, the fierce waging of the war itself is important in its own way. But (the story) takes the eagle feather" (113). In this realization, therefore, we must rethink our chastisement of Njoroge for his apparent lack of courage and down-to-earthiness in the story in which he is clearly the victim. We must try to empathize with him for being wrongly brainwashed and tenderized by the great "civilizing influence" in Africa which gave him the alphabet and the Bible and conditioned him to eschew all violence, even in self-defense. In the face of this "enlightening" crusade, how could the young Njoroge have known why the Mau Mau War of liberation is superstitious and condemnable, while "the flowers of liberty must be watered with the blood of tyrants" elsewhere on the globe?

Works cited

Achebe, Chinua. *Anthills of the Savannah,* New York: Doubleday, 1987.

Cook, David & Okenimkpe, Michael. *Ngugi wa Thjong'o:* An *Exploration of His Writings,* London: Heinemann, 1983.

Moore, Gerald. *Twelve African Writers.* Bloomington: Indiana University Press, 1980.

Ngugi, James. *Weep Not, Child.* New York: Collier Books, 1964.

Palmer, Eustace. An *Introduction to the African Novel: A Critical Study New* York: African Publishing Corporation 1972.

Pieterse, Cosmo & Duerden, Dennis. *African Writers Talking: A Collection of Radio Interviews.* N. Y.: African publishing Corp 1972.

Chapter Six

Suspense of Motif in Achebe's
Things Fall Apart

While Achebe's *Things Fall Apart* has provoked varied and significant discussions since its publication in 1958, much of the interest has focused on its protagonist, Okonkwo, and his fateful inability to grapple with change. Only incidentally have some of the discussants and critics made some peripheral comments on how suspense-filled the novel is. However, none has devoted a full-length article to suspense and its centrality in this work. This discussion is intended to fill that void. Achebe adroitly domesticates the English language, to portray the delicate orality of a non-literate culture with its dramatic imagination, to create a rich emotional tapestry of anxiety, exhilaration, anticipation and disappointment in the reader, and to make the major actions of the novel one string effectively held together by the unifying mnemonics of suspense.

Different critics and commentators have over the years applauded Achebe's language--his descriptive genius in *Things Fall Apart*. Phanuel A. Egejuru, herself an Igbo critic and writer, maintains that Achebe "has made most of the suppleness of the English language to convey the thoughts and acts of Ibo people in his writing'" (99). Emmanuel Obiechina, another Igbo critic and writer, refers to Achebe's "deliberate, systematic and sustained" use of language as his "narrative gift" (296-07). In much the same vein, Gerald Moore, one of the earliest British opinion-setters about *Things Fall Apart*, describes the novel as "extremely well-constructed, and written with confidence and precision" (59). Obviously, Moore must be talking about, among other things, Achebe's unique facility with the English language, which enabled him to produce with unobtrusive ease a book so short, but laudably communicative in its rendition of the Igbo cultural past. No wonder Donald Weinstock and Cathy Ramadan could confidently assert that Achebe's language style is "cleanly and functionally realistic" (33). This "clean" and functional aspect of suspense in *Things Fall Apart* is the subject of this discussion.

At this juncture, it is pertinent for us to refresh our understanding of the terms "suspense" and "motif," the key words of the paper's title. According to Holman, suspense is "the poised anticipation of reader or audience as to the outcome of the events of a short story, a novel, or drama, particularly as these events affect a character in the work for whom the reader or audience has formed a sympathetic attachment" (434-35). In the novel under discussion, suspense does not so much reside in "what" or "how"; the reader is sufficiently informed on these factors. Whether we are anticipating Okonkwo's self destruction, or Umuofia's killing of Ikemefuna, or the cleavage between Nwoye and his father, or the eventual conflict between the missionaries and Umuofia, the suspense resides in "when." It is this "when," this time essence that Achebe has masterfully and repeatedly manipulated through the fluidity of his language. By so doing, Achebe has elevated suspense in *Things Fall Apart* to the level of motif. In this discussion, a motif is defined as a recurrent pattern of phenomena, or events, or devices occurring by design in a work of fiction. The design is, of course, functional--to unify the different episodes of the story and to serve as a mnemonic to the reader as he tries to keep tab on events, occasions, and characters.

In Part One of *Things Fall Apart,* the tantalizing presentation of the Ikemefuna episode is artfully used as a unifying focus. In order to achieve this end, the primacy of suspense is to be established very early in the novel; hence, at the end of the first chapter, we have this suspenseful bombshell: "And that was how he came to look after the doomed lad who was sacrificed to the village of Umuofia by their neighbors to avoid war and bloodshed. The ill-fated lad was called Ikemefuna" (9). As could be noted in the above quotation, the language is aptly crafted to create suspense and heighten the reader's curiosity as to who Ikemefuna actually was. Here the reader is not preoccupied with what happened to the child, or how it happened; the author has in the passage just quoted, sensitized the reader to the child's fate through the following diction: "doomed lad," "who was sacrificed," and "the ill-fated lad." An attentive reader, at this point, would conclude that Ikemefuna was killed, but the point at which he was killed in the story is the suspense he has to discover by reading further; and that is the catch.

The "he" in the passage quoted above is, of course, Okonkwo, the protagonist in *Things Fall Apart.* So far, he is presented to us as a very successful man who has rapidly risen in his society through hard work, sheer physical strength and immovable will, in spite of his father's indolence and apparent failure in Umuofia. However, later in the novel, Achebe, through the suspenseful manipulation of the Ikemefuna episode, occasionally gives a disturbing and sinister profile of Okonkwo. As he contemplated the bone-numbing announcement by the town crier for an emergency meeting of Umuofia adult males at the market place the following morning, Okonkwo revealed his war-like instinct, and we learn the following about him:

> He was not afraid of war. He was a man of action, a
> man of war. Unlike his father he could stand the look
> of blood. In Umuofia's latest war he was the first to
> bring home a human head. That was his fifth head . . .

> On a great occasion such as the funeral of a village
> celebrity he drank his palm-wine from his first human
> head. (11)

Even the description of his physical appearance and
mannerism is equally threatening:

> He was tall and huge, and his bush eyebrows and wide
> nose gave him a very severe look . . . . When he
> walked, his heels hardly touched the ground and he
> seemed to walk on springs, as if he was going to
> pounce on somebody. And he did pounce on people
> quite often. (4)

With these inklings about Okonkwo, the reader is not
surprised to see him as the logical head of the war delegation to exert
reparations from Mbaino for killing the daughter of Umuofia.
However, Umuofia's trusting of Ikemefuna's safety in the hands of
Okonkwo in the interim must obviously continue to disturb the
reader. Will this boy-hostage be pounced upon and made miserable
before his impending fate; will he be Okonkwo's sixth human head?
And if so, when? These foreboding questions constitute the welding
torch of this first part of the novel, and they provide the impelling
urge for the reader to know the resolution. This is suspense at its best!
After introducing Ikemefuna to the reader and giving the necessary
information about him to keep the reader constantly anxious about his
well-being, Achebe then resorts to a calculated dribble. He gives only
measured information at strategic intervals in order not to rush things
and thereby offend cultural probability in this particular affair.
Achebe insinuates his reason in this matter:

> The elders of the clan had decided that Ikemefuna
> should be in Okonkwo's care for a while. But no one
> thought it would be as long as three years. They
> seemed to forget all about him as soon as they had
> taken the decision. (29)

The author then uses this lull to supply the reader some information about the seasons and farming practice, the cultural festivals and the tempo of life in Umuofia from the perspectives of key participants in the narrative, while still keeping the reader's gaze on the boy-hostage.

Achebe achieves this effective dove-tailing of event and temporal cycle at this point by using Ikemefuna's arrival at Umuofia as a measuring reference of time and events. Through this unobtrusive mnemonic, the reader is informed that:

> Ikemefuna came to Umuofia at the end of the carefree season between harvest and planting. In fact he recovered from his illness only a few days before the week of Peace began. And that was also the year Okonkwo broke the peace, and was punished, as was the custom, by Ezeani, the priest of the earth goddess. (30)

We further learn from the author's comment and from the bewildered shudder of Okonkwo's neighbors that his beating of his youngest wife, though for "justifiable anger," during the sacred week was an abomination against Ani, the earth goddess. And this offense needed cleansing by appropriate sacrifice; otherwise the clan could be ruined. As we hear from Ezeani, the prescribed placation for Okonkwo's violation includes one she-goat, one hen, a length of cloth and a hundred cowries before the shrine of Ani (30). After witnessing, as it were, this delicate orchestration of life and living at Umuofia, the reader would begin to appreciate Victor C. Uchendu's assertion that the Igbo world is "a dynamic one-a world of moving equilibrium . . . that is constantly threatened, and sometimes disturbed by natural and social calamities" and forces like antisocial behavior, homicide and the violation of taboo, "NSO or Alo" (12-13). Even in the midst of this type of functional digression, the reader is made very much aware of Ikemefuna's presence in the story. As the boy's eventual integration into Okonkwo's family life is part of the suspenseful strategy, any mention of the boy's name from this point of the story until the end of the tragic Chapter Seven is intently crafted by Achebe. With Nwoye, Okonkwo's oldest son, Ikemefuna helped Okonkwo in planting yams, the king of crops. He was equally excited about the New Yam Festival in Okonkwo's household. It was even Ikemefuna who was asked to fetch the gun with which Okonkwo fired at Ekwefi, his second wife, when she prattled "about guns that never shot" (41).

In the midst of this illusive familial comfort of Ikemefuna in Okonkwo's household, the attentive reader must grapple with some searing uncertainties, asking whether the Oracle has reprieved his death. But this is not to be. After remaining virtually silent about Ikemefuna and his affairs for a couple of chapters, the author at the beginning of Chapter Seven starts dropping some ironic and dramatic hints here and there. Now, the third year of the boy's stay at Okonkwo's household is here. As the reader has been informed earlier that no one thought that Ikemefuna's stay in Okonkwo's household would be as long as three years, the reader must be wondering where this renewed commentary on the boy is pointing. As if Achebe were preparing the "ill-fated" lad's eulogy, he is said to have grown "rapidly like a yam tendril in the rainy season" and to have been a positive influence on Okonkwo's first son Nwoye (54-55). Then dramatically, "a shadow fell on the world, and the sun seemed hidden behind a thick cloud" (58). The locusts came. What a terrible foreshadowing! Before the reader could decode these happenings, his anxiety is temporarily assuaged by a happy scene where "Okonkwo sat in his obi crunching happily with Ikemefuna and Nwoye, and drinking palm-wine copiously" (59). Achebe, in order to embrace his other stories in *Things Fall Apart,* has to abort the above euphoric scene by Ogbuefi Ezeudu's visit and warning to Okonkwo:

> That boy calls you father. Do not bear a hand in his death! . . . Yes, Umuofia has decided to kill him. The Oracle of the Hills and the Caves has pronounced it. They will take him outside Umuofia as is the custom, and kill him there. But I want you to have nothing to do with it. He calls you father. (59-60)

At this point, the reader's anxiety is no longer about when

Ikemefuna would be killed, but his concern now would be whether Okonkwo would participate in killing the boy who called him father.

Even in this circumstance, the author has from the beginning of the novel given the reader hints on what to expect from a man whose overriding fear is the fear of being perceived as weak or gentle. So, while Okonkwo's cutting down of Ikemefuna should be horrifying to the reader, it would not be surprising to him. Before putting the Ikemefuna episode to rest, the author has sufficiently informed the reader of Ogbuefi Ezeudu's qualifications for reciprocal respect and obedience in Umuofia in these terms: "Ezeudu was the oldest man in this quarter of Umuofia. He had been a great and fearless warrior in his time, and was accorded great respect in all the clan" (59). Is Achebe insinuating a repercussion on Okonkwo for not obeying the voice of age in a community where age is revered? Even Obierika's confrontation with his friend Okonkwo after the killing of Ikemefuna is more ominous:

> And let me tell you one thing, my friend. If I were you
> I would have stayed at home. What you have done
> will not please the Earth. It is the kind of action for
> which the goddess wipes out whole families. (69)

With the above cautionary insights about Okonkwo's complicity in the demise of Ikemefuna, the reader is expected to have a quick but baffling flashback to when Okonkwo's gun accidentally exploded at Ezeudu's funeral and killed the dead man's sixteen-year-old son at the end of Part One (128). The reader must be wondering whether this was coincidence or retribution. The Western reader may be inclined to opt for the former, while the Igbo is likely to see the latter as a logical sequel. Technically, the issue here is none of the above; the marvel here is how Achebe has masterfully used suspense to build connections.

While the reader, like the Umuofia crowd, is still drained and anguished by this accidental killing of Ezeudu's son at his father's funeral, Achebe uses the gap provided by the pandemonium to give the reader a lesson in Umuofia traditional ordinance. According to this ordinance:

The only course to Okonkwo was to flee from the
clan. It was a crime against the earth goddess to kill a
clansman, and a man who committed it must flee from
the land. The crime was of two kinds. male and
female.
Okonkwo had committed the female, because it had
been inadvertent. He could return to the clan after
seven years. (128-129)

In compliance with this ritual, Okonkwo and his family fled
to his motherland, a little village called Mbanta (129). At this point,
the reader must be wondering if this actually happened to Okonkwo,
the successful and strong man of Umuofia. Achebe in turn must be
saying, "yes" and reminding the reader, in the words of David Carroll,
that in Igboland, "the individual cannot be allowed an absolutism
which is denied even to his chi. Man's uniqueness and independence
is curtailed in fact, by the will of his community . . . "(18). The reader
is given this insight as a signpost to guide his speculations and
fashion his anxieties.

As the reader contemplates what type of reception Okonkwo
would be accorded in his motherland, the reader must simultaneously
wonder what Umuofia would be like in the absence of its strong man;
how Nwoye would fair in exile with his father after the tragic killing
of his mentor, Ikemefuna, would be equally on the reader's mind.
Achebe uses the next six chapters, which constitute Part Two of
Things Fall Apart, to respond to these preoccupations. After making
the reader a witness to the cordial and nerve-calming reception
Uchendu gave to his nephew, Okonkwo, by making land available to
him to build huts for himself and his wives and by the old man's
words of advice and encouragement, the author then ingeniously
responds to the reader's two other concerns.

Using Obierika, Okonkwo's best friend, as plausible liaison
between Umuofia and Mbanta, Achebe gives the reader some insight
into what was afoot in both clans, thereby maintaining fusion in his
plot. Obierika's first visit to his friend at Mbanta was fraught with
suspense and ominous insinuations, even though its purpose was
generous and thoughtful--he came to see Okonkwo and bring him the

money from the sale of his yams. After the customary salutation, the men settled down to drink palm-wine and indulge themselves with yarns. Incidentally, Okonkwo's uncle, Uchendu, braggingly included Abame in the catalogue of places he had visited in his heyday. At the mention of Abame, Obierika asked the banal question: "Have you heard that Abame is no more?" (142). As Okonkwo and Uchendu could not understand how the assertion in the above question could be true, Obierika had to explain: "Abame has been wiped out. It is a strange and terrible story . . ." (142). By doling out his information with strategic pauses, Obierika creates tension and anxiety in his audience as well as in the reader. In summary, according to his story, the Abame people had killed a stray white man and were brutally massacred on their market day under the order of three white men. The Oracle had earlier warned the Abame people that "other white men were on their way. They were locusts . . . and the first man was their harbinger sent to explore the terrain" (143).

At this point, the reader would anxiously recall that the locusts came earlier in the story and foreshadowed the killing of Ikemefuna and Okonkwo's subsequent problem at Ezeudu's funeral. His question now would be, what will the white men referred to as "locusts" bring to Okonkwo in particular and Umuofia in general?

Okonkwo's response to Obierika's story matches his characteristic profile of being rash and physical. He called the Abame people fools for not arming themselves with guns and machetes to defend themselves against the white men, even when the Oracle had warned them (145). Through such hints, Achebe is preparing the reader for Okonkwo's impending confrontation with his son, Nwoye, for patronizing the white man's religion, which would rear its head during Obierika's second visit to Mbanta. Obierika's rejoinder to his friend's statement above is indeed sobering:

> They had paid for their foolishness . . . But I am afraid. We have heard stories about white men who made the powerful guns and strong drinks and took slaves away across the seas, but no one thought the stories were true. (145)

The implication of the above observation could be fairly surmised by the reader--the white man is on the march to Umuofia and its environs. But what is in store for Okonkwo and his temperament? This is the suspense--the reader's anxiety, his anticipation.

As far back as Chapter Two, where Nwoye is portrayed as being twelve years old, his father has already started to be perversely worried over what he perceived as the boy's feebleness and apparent femininity. In Chapter Eight, after Okonkwo had already ironically killed Ikemefuna, who had started to be a positive role-model for Nwoye in Chapter Seven, Okonkwo is complaining and asking: "Where are the young suckers that will grow when the old banana tree dies?" (68). Of course, he is referring to his male children, especially to Nwoye.

So far, Achebe has strategically put in place the emotional explosives needed to start the blaze which would, as it were, burn down Umuofia's totem of cultural and political autonomy and facilitate the cleavage between father and son foreshadowed very early in the novel. What is needed at this point is the right friction here and there to activate these tinder boxes. At this point in the novel, Chapter Sixteen, that is, events and temper would be racing as forest fires to some tragic and irredeemable conclusion. Immediately the reader learns from the author that Obierika's second visit to Mbanta was not a happy one, a string of distending revelations follows:

> The missionaries had come to Umuofia. They had
> built their church there, won a handful of converts and
> were already sending evangelists to the surrounding
> towns and villages. That was a source of great sorrow
> to the leaders of the clan. (147)

With the above revelations the reader's anticipation of Umuofia's collective catastrophe is systematically falling in place. While he would still be thinking about the relationship between Okonkwo and his son, Nwoye, the reader might not be anticipating anything dramatic soon in this regard. But as Achebe makes it clear that "what

moved Obierika to visit Okonkwo was the sudden appearance of . .
. Nwoye, among the missionaries in Umuofia" and his baffling
denunciation of his father before Obierika, the reader then sits up to
embrace Okonkwo's response. Ironically, Obierika's story to
Okonkwo does not produce the bang the reader has anticipated
because it is only a sequel to what happened earlier in Mbanta before
Obierika arrived. The reader is told that "Okonkwo did not wish to
speak about Nwoye" and that "it was only from Nwoye's mother that
he [Obierika] heard scraps of the story" (148). It is in Chapter
Seventeen that the author fills the reader in on the story itself.
Okonkwo has been told by one of his maternal cousins that his son,
Nwoye, was among the Christians. Then Okonkwo acted in a typical
fashion; he sprang to his feet and attacked the boy, choking and
beating him. Achebe allows the reader to experience the terror of this
menacing attack from the boy's point of view. From this point, Nwoye
walked away from his father and never returned. When the reader
learns that

> he went back to the church and told Mr. Kiaga that he
> had decided to go to Umuofia where the white
> missionary had set up a school to teach young
> Christians to read and write, (157)

the reader is not surprised at all at this decision and final break
between father and son; he has anxiously anticipated it for a long
time. The reader by now must have no doubt sensed that this
irrevocable severance of filial ties is one of the things that have fallen
apart in the novel. The Western reader may feel at this point some
exhilaration for the triumph of the individual spirit over a repressive
force represented by Okonkwo, while the African will surely bemoan
the loss of the age-honored tradition of respect for age.

Jonathan Peter's observation about Achebe's aim in writing
Things Fall Apart becomes a logical imperative. According to Peters,
Achebe "wanted, first of all, to evoke the pattern of life in a
traditional African setting, notably its order, harmony, poetry and
beauty for the benefit of the younger generation" (97). As the reader
follows Okonkwo home to Umuofia after the seven futile years of

exile, he would obviously notice "Umuofia had indeed changed" (180). Not only had the church been firmly established in the clan, but "the white man had also brought a government . . . [and] had built a court where the District Commissioner judged cases in ignorance . . ." (181). This, of course, is the voice of Obierika, who was briefing his friend after his fateful return to Umuofia. Okonkwo learned about the court messengers who brought men to the white man for trial, about men of title being thrown into prison and made to do menial jobs, about the abrogation of native laws and customs in favor of the white man's law, and about other horrible and inciteful acts like the hanging of Aneto for killing a kinsman. Achebe has crafted the dialogue between Obierika and Okonkwo in Chapter Twenty in a subtle and precisional manner to produce charged tension in temperamental Okonkwo and to impel the reader to anticipate some disaster. The reader is, however, reminded that Umuofia would never muster united front against the white man. When Okonkwo wondered why his people had "lost the power to fight" and decided, "We must fight these men and drive them from the land," his friend's response that "it is already too late" reflects the people's consensus (182). Through Obierika's rhetorical question, "How do you think we can fight when our own brothers have turned against us?" (183), the reader is made to speculate that Okonkwo would be on his own should he choose to fight.

To set the stage for the final and dramatic show-down of the novel, Achebe has to orchestrate the immediate departure of the moderate and level-headed missionary, Mr. Brown, from Umuofia and his replacement by the rash and racist Mr. Smith. As the reader contemplates the impending tragedy in the fateful mix of Okonkwo and Mr. Smith in Umuofia, Enoch, one of the brash and perverted converts, has "thrown Umuofia into confusion" by unmasking an Egwugwu, thereby killing "an ancestral spirit." For days the air was heavily charged with tension, which culminated in the burning of Mr. Smith's church (193-97). The reader, who learned about what happened to the Abame people several months after they had killed one white man, must be edgy at this church-burning incident, and this anxiety is not in vain. Three days after this incident, the District Commissioner in Umuru committed a series of breaches of faith against Umuofia by summoning six of her elders, including Okonkwo, to his headquarters, disarming and imprisoning them under false pretense, until ransom was paid for their release.

As Umuofia gathered as a body for the last time in the novel "to speak its mind about the things that were happening" (205), Achebe speaks to the reader in riddling terms. The author's intentional equivocation is meant to baffle the reader and guard against omniscient conclusions on his part. By way of preamble, the reader is made privy to Okonkwo's thinking and resolve on his way to the meeting with his friend Obierika. The reader learns of Okonkwo's decision to fight alone, if it would come to that, and of his greatest fear--Egonwanne, the restraining orator of Umuofia. At the meeting, Okika, the first keynote speaker, had started to give a very compelling emotional speech which was strategically punctuated by untying rhetorical questions. For example, he says:

> This is a great gathering. No clan can boast of greater numbers of great valor. But are we all here? I ask you: Are all the sons of Umuofia with us here? They are not . . . . If we fight the stranger we shall hit our brothers and perhaps shed the blood of a clansman. But we must do it. Our fathers never dreamed of such a thing, they never killed their brothers. But a white man never came to them. So we must do what our fathers would never have done . . . . We must bale this water now that it is only ankle deep. (209-10)

In the midst of Okika's speech, several court messengers came to disrupt the meeting. In one of the most powerful dramatic acts in the novel, Okonkwo beheaded the leader of the interlopers. Although the reader is now left drained by the sheer brutality and thoughtlessness of Okonkwo's final act, the reader could not readily blame him for Umuofia's ineffectiveness in dealing with the white man. Evidently, had the meeting continued undisturbed, other notable orators like Egonwanne, the sweet-coated crowd-puller feared by Okonkwo, would have spoken to deflate Okika's call to arms. It was this uncertainty that drove Okonkwo to hang himself afterwards in his backyard.

As the novel ends the way it does, the reader is left only with inferential conclusions about Umuofia and its relationship with the white man, but not about Umuofia as a people and as a culture. The author has made it clear that the clan had dignity, order, harmony and autonomy before the white man gained entrance to its gate through the back door of missionary fervor. As nothing was resolved or resolvable then about this contact--this relationship--the story of the novel is trying to recreate, it would be artistically implausible for the author to presume a moral solution. What Achebe has done, and superbly so, is to carve a living story out of this immovable cloud of suspense which anthropologists refer to as culture-contact.

WORKS CITED

Achebe, Chinua. *Things Fall Apart*. New York: Astor Honor, Inc, 1959.

Carroll, David. *Chinua Achebe*. New York: St. Martins Press, 1980.

Egejuru, Phanuel A. *Black Writer: White Audience*. New York: Exposition Press, 1978.

Holman, Hugh C. *A Handbook to Literature*. Indianapolis: The Bobb Merrill Company, Inc, 1980.

Moore, Gerald. *Seven African Writers*. London: Oxford University Press, 1962.

Obiechina, Emmanuel. *Culture, Tradition* and *Society in the West African Novel*. London: Cambridge University Press, 1975.

Peters, Jonathan. *A Dance of Masks: Senghor, Achebe, Soyinka*. Washington, D. C.: Three Continents Press, 1978.

Uchendu, Victor C. *The Igbo of Southeast Nigeria.* New York: Northwestern University, 1965.

Weinstock, Donald, and Cathy Ramadan. "Symbolic Structure in *Things Fall Apart." Critique: Studies in Modern Fiction* 2: 33-41.

Chapter Seven

Satiric Candor in *The Fire Next Time*

In reading the various and pertinent criticisms, comments, and observations about the illustrious author, the late James Baldwin, the present writer discovered a consistent unanimity on two aspects of his works. The first is that, for Baldwin, writing is a functional instrument--a medium of social criticism. The second refers to his impeccable sincerity of expression. Specifically, in *The Fire Next Time,* the element of social criticism is intact; however, the author is not merely interested in trashing his society for its errors and omissions. He is inviting it, instead, to look at itself and reason with him in order for both to avoid a collective disaster.

It is important, for the sake of clarity, for us to put the two words of the title of this essay, "Satiric Candor," in perspective. In his *A Handbook to Literature,* Holman defines "satire" as "a literary manner which blends a critical attitude with humor and wit for the purpose of improving human institutions or humanity" (398). "Candor," as defined by *The American Heritage Dictionary of the*

English Language (The New College Edition), is "frankness of expression; sincerity, straightforwardness [and] freedom from prejudice." It also sees satire as "a literary work in which irony, derision, or wit in any form is used to expose folly or wickedness." Anyone who reads *The Fire Next Time* with perception will necessarily concede that it exhibits many, if not all, of the characteristics of satire espoused by these definitions. Baldwin's *The Fire Next Time* is characteristically his own brand of satire, freely combining the essential ingredients of Juvenalian and Horatian schools: moral indignation and corrective censure (Holman 399).

Baldwin's deliberate probing of our collective psyche to expose our follies and presumptions challenges our sensibilities and tests our fairness. Through his abrasive candor and forthrightness, he disarms our resistance and compels our attention whether we like it or not. This line of thinking is underscored by Standley in his discussion of James Baldwin's incessant currency in these terms:

> Baldwin's works have never lacked audience. The rationale for this public interest in his works obviously consists of multiple factors, among them being his prophetic tone, moral concern, . . . perceptive relevance, intense language, and poignant sincerity. (15)

Certainly, Baldwin's "perceptive relevance, intense language and poignant sincerity" fuel the engine of his satiric stance in *The Fire Next Time.* Even the title of the book itself is fraught with warning; if we do not listen to the author, a fellow human being, maybe we might heed the imminence of the contractual doom referred to in this biblical allusion--God's promise to Noah after the "Deluge."

As it has been observed earlier in this discussion, Baldwin, in his own brand of satire in *The Fire Next Time,* employs corrective censure and moral indignation to castigate the malignant social evil of his society--racism, and its attendant off-shoots, group suspicion and hate. He has no apology to offer to anyone for the stance he has taken in the two autobiographical essays of the book under discussion. As an artist who sees writing as a functional instrument of social criticism, Baldwin could not be complacent and complimentary, while things are flying out the window in his society. After all, Baldwin's role is a very defined one, and there is no dilemma about his subject matter. He puts it this way in one of his interviews edited by Standley and Pratt: "I am an American writer. This country is my subject" (viii). No one will doubt that *The Fire Next Time* is characteristically American in content and tempo. Baldwin's stance in this book is that something is glaringly wrong in his society, in this bastion of "liberty" and "human rights," and that some one has to damn the consequences and take the bull by the horn in order to call the spectators' (his fellow Americans') attention to their collective danger.

Using the autobiographical letter to his nephew, entitled "My Dungeon Shook," as a dialectical preamble, Baldwin chides the calculated inadvertency with which America has systematically tried to squeeze African-Americans out of existence in their own country. As the author reasons with his nephew, who might be any black youth, on the reality of being black in America, he profiles the nephew's father, who might also be any adult black male. This profile is Baldwin's ammunition, his satire on the society that produced and made the nephew's father a living mask. He observes:

> But no one's hand can wipe away those tears he sheds invisibly today, which one hears in his laughter and in his songs . . . and this is the crime of which I accuse my country and my countrymen, for which neither I, nor time, nor history will ever forgive them, that they have destroyed and are destroying hundreds of thousands of lives and do not know it and do not want to know it . . . . But it is not permissible that the authors of devastation should also be innocent. It is the innocence which constitutes the . . . crime. (15-16)

This observation is incontestable; it is bold and sincere and uttered without malice or prejudice. It is meant to give the American readership food-for-thought and provoke its common sense. It is the voice of righteous indignation--the reformist's outcry at social and moral wrongs. In his new book, entitled *James Baldwin: Artist on Fire,* 1989, W. J. Weatherby, a prize-winning journalist and novelist, comments on Baldwin's veracity in these terms:

> . . . in the U.S. today there is not another writer, white or black, who expresses with such poignancy and abrasiveness the . . . realities of the racial ferment in North and South. (205)

Still addressing his nephew on the "innocents," Baldwin assumes the ironic stance--the characteristic mode of satire--to excoriate the evasive complacency of his countrymen and women, which has created and sustained "The Tale of Two Cities" in a land which is supposed to be opulent and urbane:

> Now, my dear namesake, these innocents and well-meaning people, your countrymen, have caused you to be born under conditions not very far removed from the London of more than a hundred years ago. (16)

In this section of *The Fire Next Time,* Baldwin sees his task as the sharpening of consciousness in his nephew--in every black youth, to embrace life with fortitude in an impervious land because, for Baldwin and his people, survival is an imperative. He writes, "And you must survive because we love you, and for the sake of your children and your children's children" (17). The pathos invoked in the above sentiment indirectly exposes and implicitly ridicules the inhumanity of the system that subjects its youth to excruciating existence just because of the color of their skin.

The author then clarifies his admonition to his nephew and, by implication, further censures the immorality of a country that would deliberately continue to make the humanity of many of her citizens an issue of debate in the second half of the twentieth century. What lends credence and virulence to Baldwin's revelation to his kin is the candor--the sincerity in which it is couched. No word is minced; no camouflage is intended. He unequivocally explains:

You were born where you were born and faced the
future that you faced because you were black and for
no other reason. The limits of your ambition were,
thus, expected to be set forever. You were born into a
society which spelled out with brutal clarity, and in as
many ways as possible, that you were a worthless
human being. (18)

In his capacity as a social critic--satirists are social critics--
Baldwin shows that he, as he, per duty, tears down the moribund
racial fence with its confining strictures, has a moral responsibility to
create an enduring openness. He does not conclude this section of the
book without ensuring the existence of an open oasis of ideas and
untrammeled brotherhood, where his nephew, James, and others
would, together, build a better America--a better world. He does just
that in this injunction:

Please try to be clear, dear James, through the storm
which rages about your youthful head toady, about
the reality which lies behind the words acceptance and
integration. There is no reason for you to try to
become like white people and there is no basis
whatever for their assumption that they must accept
you. The really terrible thing, old buddy, is that you
must accept them. And I mean that very seriously.
You must accept them with love . . . . (19)

The above injunction is relevantly explicated in Burney J.
Hollis' tribute to James Baldwin in *The Sun* of December 2, 1987, in
these terms:

He [Baldwin] realized . . . that blacks must arrive at
self-acceptance and self-love as a precondition for
accepting whites with love and that whites need to rid
themselves of self-deception if they are to achieve
racial harmony. (B-5)

The abiding role of a satirist or social critic is to infuse understanding and the exercise of common sense in his audience, his readers. He may achieve this task through a number of ways. First, he must choose to strike out the effrontery in his target through some preposterous agenda, as it is the case with Swift's "Modest Proposal," or he may elect the route of critical praise tinged with philosophical explanation. Baldwin, in his attempt to explain to his nephew the reasons why his white countrymen react the way they do toward him and other blacks, finds ammunition in the latter. He offers the following observation:

Many of them, indeed know better, but, as you will discover, people find it very difficult to act on what they know. To act is to be committed, and to be committed is to be in danger. (20)

This barb of conscience, this paradoxical and biting candor, is intended to jostle both black and white Americans out of their mutual stupor of racial suspicion and hate through the liberating act of mutual tolerance and forebearance. Baldwin, in this autobiographical letter to his nephew, has vindicated his stated view that "the artist cannot and must not take anything for granted, but drive to the heart of every answer and expose the question the answer hides" (Standley 16). In this first part of *The Fire Next Time,* Baldwin has done what he has undertaken to do: to tell the truth to his nephew, as he perceives it, to offend or ridicule, when it is necessary, at the side of the truth, in short, to put before us the moral dilemma of our celebrating the one hundredth anniversary of the "Emancipation Proclamation," while the shackles are still in place.

Having put the paradoxical existence of the secular system of his society in an unmistakable perspective, in the foregone section, Baldwin then turns his searing candor to organized religion and its pandering subservience to power, hate and greed. This section of *The Fire Next Time* is entitled "Down at the Cross: Letter From a Region in My Mind." The title is fraught with irony, and the content is laced with sarcasm. It is a cogently deliberate piece of literature intended to baffle the complacent and lend ammunition to the moral indignation

addressed to anyone who has any presumption to Christian faith or to
any religion at all. In other words, "Down at the Cross" is a dialectic
on social inequities in a supposedly "Christian Nation," and it exposes
religious intolerance and exemplifies moral courage.

In this section, Baldwin does not spare the church for its
complicity with the secular system of society in keeping blacks in
their "place." By way of satiric insinuation on the ironic implication
of the phrase "Christian Nation," Baldwin purposely retrospects into
his boyhood years of the 1930s, in Harlem. He talks about his
euphoric flight into the church for safety: "And since I had been born
in a Christian nation, I accepted this Deity as the only one . . . . 1 also
supposed that God and safety were synonymous" (27). Taking us, the
readers, by the hand, as it were, Baldwin reviews the heroic and albeit
debilitating experience of growing up for the black youth in Harlem,
"the metropolis of grief," as Donald Barr would put it. And before we
could ask why life is so bleak and uninspiring for the black youth in
Harlem, Baldwin in his characteristic bluntness observes:

> One did not have to be very bright to realize how little
> one could do to change one's situation; one did not
> have to be abnormally sensitive to be worn down to a
> cutting edge by the incessant gratuitous humiliation
> and danger one encountered every working day, all
> day long. (32)

Of course, Baldwin, in the above passage, refers to the racial
taunting directed toward the blacks of his youth at their places of
work. Since there is nothing to inspire hope, a sense of belonging and
faith in them, the Harlem youth, according to Baldwin, resort to crime
as a morale booster. He explains:

> Crime became real,--for the first time--not as a
> possibility. One would never defeat one's
> circumstance by working and saving one's pennies;
> one would never, by working, acquire that many
> pennies and besides the social treatment accorded
> even the most successful Negroes proved that one

needed, in order to be free, something more than a bank account. One needed a handle, a lever, a means of inspiring fear. (33-34)

The satire in the above two references is implicit. Baldwin, in his role as a social critic, "the incorrigible disturber of peace," wants us to wonder and shudder. When we ask ourselves then why a citizen of a rich and "Christian Nation" should be driven by his countrymen and women to such extreme routes to earn human dignity, we shall have imbibed and heeded Baldwin's moral caution, that man's inhumanity to man negates the apparent decency of our civilization.

As an even-handed satirist, Baldwin spares nobody--not even himself and his boyhood affiliation with the church in his vehement opposition to social inequalities and religious hypocrisy. He chides and ridicules the social milieu that has created and continues to condone the burgeoning economic disparity between the blacks and their white counterparts. In much the same vein, he casts an eye of disapproval against any blacks who would rob white people without any scruple. About his boyhood ministry, he tells us that his entrance into the church was not for vocation but for selfish ends--to avoid being involved in crime or becoming a statistic of the same, and he does not mince words in letting us know that many Christians out there have their own private and opposing agenda from Christ's. This "uncommon honesty," as Hollis states, has made Baldwin's voice a compelling one.

Even if some or many of his audience or readers, individually or in groups, may feel inexorably tense or abashed at his incessant plucking on their personal or collective shames, Baldwin knows he must continue to annoy and to make uneasy because his constructive intentions of reforming his society must preclude complacency. Ideally, Baldwin continues to laugh at us and with us about the mighty institution we call the church. He had been there and knows the ropes. Using his experiences as an erstwhile church "insider," he castigates the church and her Christians for their misinformation and misapplication of religion. He writes:

. . . the principles governing the rites and customs of

the churches in which I grew up did not differ from
the principles governing the rites and customs of other
churches, white. The principles were Blindness,
Loneliness, and Terror,--I would love to believe that
the principles were Faith, Hope and Charity, but this
is clearly not so for most Christians, or for what we
call the Christian world. (47)

What is this blindness, this loneliness, this terror, in a
supposedly holy institution whose injunction is to spread Faith, Hope
and Charity among human beings? Baldwin offers a scalding
illustration of the blindness of which he speaks in the passage above.
He satirically declares:

Being in the pulpit is like being in a theatre; I was behind the
scenes and knew how the illusion was worked. I knew the
other ministers and knew the quality of their lives--I knew
how to work on a congregation until the last dime was
surrendered-it was not very hard to do--and I knew where the
money for "the lord's work" went. (55-56)

This observation is a comical, yet serious indictment of
organized religion for creating an illusion of faith for the personal
enrichment of "God's relatives." Turning to the paradoxical
association of the church with "terror," Baldwin ridicules organized
religion and its adherents for merely being interested in the
acquisition and preservation of turfs--hence their divide-and-rule
tactics:

In the same way that we, for white people, were the
descendants of Ham and were cursed forever, while people
were, for us, the descendants of Cain. And the passion with
which we love the Lord was a measure of how deeply we
feared and distrusted and, in the end, hated almost all
strangers, always, and avoided and despised ourselves. (59)

The third principle governing the church, as Baldwin

perceives it from his some-time "insider" angle, is Loneliness. The author, of course, refers to the loneliness of the spirit that molests any church adherent with the moral gumption to sense or question the apparent contradictions in the teachings of the church about the goodness of the Christian God and the bliss of eternal life. Through his adroit use of language to give immediacy to his anguished perception of the realities around him then as a boy minister of the church in Harlem, Baldwin pricks the collective conscience of his "Christian nation" in the following observation:

> When I watched all the children, their copper, brown, and beige faces staring up at me as I taught Sunday school, I felt that I was committing a crime in talking about the gentle Jesus, in telling them to reconcile themselves to their misery on earth in order to gain the crown of eternal life. Were only Negroes to gain this crown? Was Heaven, then, to be merely another ghetto? (57)

In this passage, Baldwin ingeniously leaves some questions unasked. It is left to us, the readers, to ask them. Here lies the irony of Baldwin's satire against the church. He asks through our questions: "Did Jesus not first feed the hungry and heal the sick before preaching the gospel to them? What is the Church doing to alleviate human misery in the Harlem ghetto?" Although these are disconcerting questions that Baldwin puts into our mouths, they are enlightening and liberating. For those who may be inclined to dismiss our author as too contentious and inciting, Dryden's admonition about the responsibility of satire is incisively applicable:

> The true end of satyr, is the amendment of vice by correction. And he who writes Honestly, is no more an Enemy to the Offendour, than the Physician to the Patient, when he prescribes harsh Remedies to an inveterate Disease . . . . (Winn 353)

After all, Baldwin's expressed philosophy about his art is that the writer has a moral responsibility to contend with his society, in order to help shape and straighten it when it is necessary (Standley 16).

Nowhere in *The Fire Next Time* is Baldwin's consistency as a social critic--a writer with a healing mission--so rigorously put to the test as in his handling of the Nation of Islam's agenda for black people in America. This test reaches its climax in his invitation to the Honorable Elijah Muhammad's Chicago South Side mansion (80). Will he condemn religious intolerance in the Christian church with such moral intensity as we previously discussed in this paper, and connive at or condone it in the black Mosque? Will Baldwin expose and ridicule the misapplication of religion by Christians and allow a free reign to the Nation of Islam? Will candor be thrown out in the guest's civil attempt to appease his host? None of the above questions receives an affirmative response in *The Fire Next Time*.

While Baldwin appreciated the racial and social intransigencies that gave birth to Islam and lent credence to its teachings among many blacks in the United States, he refuses to subscribe to its new empowerment indoctrination that "[a]ll black men belong to Islam" or that "they have been chosen. And Islam shall rule the world" (80). He also refuses to see all white people as sinners and enemies (93). As the satirist eschews bitterness or blind revenge, his self-giving role is to extricate his society, his fellow countrymen and women from the banal effrontery of self-destruction. He accomplishes this task through the regulated and persistent ridicule of his poignant pen. This is true of Baldwin in his satiric stance in *The Fire Next Time*. He unequivocally rejects the Nation of Islam's philosophy that "[t]hey segregate us, we segregate them." Maintaining the incorruptible independence of the satirist--the social critic, Baldwin, in his characteristic sincerity, observes:

> I am very much concerned that American Negroes achieve their freedom here in the United States. But I am also concerned for their dignity, for the health of their souls, and must oppose any attempt that Negroes may make to do to others what has been done to them. (113)

From the above stance, Baldwin, as the artist, recognizes his theatre of operation as the human canvas. He must continue to be an impartial teacher of his society--of mankind. It is no wonder, therefore, that he concludes *The Fire Next Time* with a plea for moral conscience--moral courage on the part of his countrymen and women, black and white, to forestall "the racial nightmare" and salvage America for themselves and posterity or face the imperative of collective annihilation by fire, as promised to Noah in the Bible (141).

As we have seen from our discussion, *The Fire Next Time* is a small but very compelling book. Baldwin's friend William Styron sees the book as "one of the great documents of the 20th century." John Henrick Clarke, as quoted by Standley in his study entitled "James Baldwin," affirms that the book was probably instrumental "in restoring the personal essay to its place as a form of creative literature" (20). It is also highly likely that Burney J. Hollis was thinking about the impact of *The Fire Next* Time on contemporary America when he observed that "Mr. Baldwin was one of the most powerful and compelling American writers of the 20th century (5-B). It is needless to say that the book is all of the above because of the stance and skill of its author: his moral indignation and corrective censure, coupled with his uncanny sincerity of expression. In this little book, Baldwin has compelled America to look at itself; he has set America on the road to becoming an inclusive society. Because of these, his legacy is a solid one. He lived his perennial caution. He was never a hater of persons, but of the evil within.

WORKS CITED

Barr, Donald."Guilt Was Everywhere." *New York Times Book Review* (May 17, 1963), 5. Reprinted in *James Baldwin: A Reference Guide,* Ed. Fred L. Standley and V. Nancy Standley. Boston: G. K. Hall & Co., 1980.

Baldwin, James. *The Fire Next Time.* New York: Dell Publishing Company, Inc., 1963.

Hollis, Burney J. "An Apostle of Truth: James Arthur Baldwin." *The*

Baltimore Sun, December 2, 1987, B-5.

Holman, Hugh C. *A Handbook to Literature.* 4th ed. Indianapolis: The Bob Merrill Company, Inc., 1980.

Standley, Fred L. "James Baldwin." *Dictionary of Literary Biography.* 2 vols. Detroit: Gale Research Company, 1989.

Standley, Fred L., and Louis H. Pratt, *eds. Conversation with James Baldwin.* Jackson, Mississippi: University Press of Mississippi, 1989.

Weatherby, W. J. *James Baldwin: Artist on Fire.* New York: Donald J. Fine, Inc., 1989.

Winn, James Anderson. *John Dryden and His World.* New Haven: Yale University Press, 1987.

Chapter Eight

Contrapuntal Characters in Achebe's *Things Fall Apart*

For almost four decades, *Things Fall Apart*, Achebe's maiden novel, has deservedly gathered and continues to garner encomiums from around the world. Variously described as "an extremely well-constructed short novel" (Gerald Moore 59); as assuredly deserving "its universal fame" (Eustance Palmer 63); and as "the best first novel since the war" (Dr. Macrae, quoted in *Homenews* 11), Achebe's novel derives its enduring appellations from its manifold features--among them, its author's consistent refusal to explain, defend or justify anything in the novel but to tell his story through the even-handed portrayal of his characters, both native and foreign. To ensure this objective stance and also guard against any sweeping categorization of the African, Achebe employs the scheme of contrapuntal characterization as a functional device in *Things Fall Apart*.

It is through this pairing of opposites--this juxtaposition of contraries that Achebe tells us about the tradition and custom of Igbo land in retrospect before the disruptive impact of European missionaries and colonialists on its autonomy and social fabrics. As we encounter the main characters--the key players in this epic tale of ancient values and dignity, personal triumphs and disappointments, and albeit, mutual suspicion engendered by human frailties and instincts, we shall be mindful of their individual differences which explain their disparate responses to life and events in the novel. Let us take Okonkwo, the hero of the novel, for instance. By all accounts, he is a very plausible figure: convincing in his portrayal as a man of action, and credible in his role as one of the elders of his clan. However, Okonkwo's rise to fame and opulence is as phenomenal as it is precipitous. It is the former because his material greatness has shattered controversies in Umuofia and beyond, because of its solid foundations and demonstrable nature, in spite of his father's indolence and material deficit. Achebe emphasizes the above facts thus:

> Okonkwo was well known throughout the nine villages of Umuofia and even beyond. His fame rested on solid personal achievements. (3)
> . . . he had won fame as the greatest wrestler in the nine villages. He was a wealthy farmer and had two barns full of yams, and had just married his third wife. To crown it all he had taken two titles. (8-9)
> Okonkwo did not have the start in life which many young men usually had. He did not inherit a barn from his father. There was no barn to inherit. (17)

It is the latter because it is greatness achieved and continuously propped by sheer physical strength and callous ambition. To underscore this side of Okonkwo and thereby hint at the tragic makeup of his fortune, the author compares Okonkwo's fame to "a bush-fire in the harmattan"[season]; he is said to have "no patience with unsuccessful men" (4). We are also informed that "he was a very strong man and rarely felt fatigue," hence his wives and children suffered because of his dawn-to-bedtime approach to farming (15).

At this point one would normally ask: "What is wrong with being strong and working hard?" Achebe in *Things Fall Apart* does not say or imply that anything is wrong with these experiences. However, with Okonkwo's streak of experience, the author introduces a tragic dimension in the hero's psychology with the following observation:

> But his whole life was dominated by fear, the fear of failure and weakness . . . It was not external but lay deep within himself. It was the fear of himself, lest he should be found to resemble his father (14).

In the light of the above revelation, any accurate assessment of Okonkwo's success or failure must derive from our examination of his response to this fear in relation to events and other people, and from his peers' individual profiles and responses to the same or comparable events or experiences. This approach is contrapuntal in essence and conforms to Achebe's design in *Things Fall Apart*.

As Okonkwo's source of fear and insecurity is his father's profile, let us examine father and son side by side to see whether this fear is normal or psychotic, within the framework of Umuofia's culture. Unoka, Okonkwo's father is portrayed as a complete failure materially; he could not even provide enough food for his wife and children. What makes Unoka's situation preposterous in Umuofia's traditional setting is that it is self-inflicted due to his laziness and tomorrowlessness which make him an inveterate debtor, and object of laughter in the clan. Even he is a coward in a culture where manly courage is an admired quality (4-7). Normally, any son whether he is from Umuofia or any other place on earth where materialism is a determining factor in life, would like to rise above his father's circumstance, especially if his father's is not reassuring.

We have already recognized Okonkwo's fame, his personal achievements and filial disadvantages. We rejoice that he is able to achieve in spite of the latter, but we cringe at his preoccupation with over-proving himself and clinging to the tragic memory of a dead father. For him to eschew idleness--his father's indigent trait, is a normal inclination, but for Okonkwo to make the rejection of his father's gentleness a passion is indeed self-destructing and uncalled for (15). Even Umuofia as a people and culture applaud and recognize personal achievements and leadership qualities and do not base their appraisal of a man on his father's identity (80). As a result of this cultural dispensation, and because of Okonkwo's personal achievements, he becomes at a very young age one of the elders of Umuofia and logical custodian of the boy-hostage, Ikemefuna (9). In the light of these internal evidence, the following questions become inevitable: Why should a man like Okonkwo whose physical strength and solid personal achievements have been recognized and universally hailed by his clan and beyond be gingerly consumed by the past? Why should a man who knew poverty and hard times exude impatience and derision at less successful men?

As we have inferred above, the answer to these two questions lies in Okonkwo's ingrained opposition to his father's qualities including even his positive--gentleness and aesthetic appreciation of his surrounding, which Eustace Palmer believes Okonkwo "would have been the better for possessing" (55). To put the above observation in perspective, let us refer to the portrayal of father and son in the novel in regard to their respective temperaments. Let's begin with Okonkwo's:

> When he walked, his heels hardly touched the ground and he seemed to walk on springs, as if he was going to pounce on somebody. And he did pounce on people quite often. He had a slight stammer and whenever he was angry and could not get his words out quickly enough, he would use his fists. He had no patience with unsuccessful men. He had had no patience with his father (4).

On Unoka's side, we have already documented his laziness, spendthrift, indebtedness and his inability to feed his family, but we have yet to profile his gentle aspects. He is said to be a good flute player, who loved fellowship and good food. Whenever he played the flute his face would beam with blessedness and peace. As an itinerant musician, Unoka played the role of a teacher and preserver of cultural aesthetics (6-7). From the above profiles, we could see that Okonkwo lacks his father's gentler nature, or as the novel indicates, he is passionately suppressing it (7).

It is this unfortunate embargo on gentleness that sets Okonkwo nihilistically apart from his son Nwoye and his best friend, Obierika and Ezeudu--a revered elder in Umuofia. It is this "neurotic streak in his character", as Emmanuel Obiechina describes it, that "carries him beyond the limits of common standards" (93).

Now let us pair Okonkwo and his best friend, Obierika, for it is Achebe's design that we resist the temptation of regarding Okonkwo as a representative Umuofian or its macrocosmic referent, Igbo. In fact, the contrapuntal nature in these two friends' characterization begins with the meaning and sound of their respective names. As some of us know, Igbo is a tonal language; this means that the meaning of a word is usually inherent in its sound. For example, note how unobtrusively the word, Obi-eri-ka sounds to the ear. Linguistically, the name"Obierika" means the home of the multitude. Is it any wonder then that Okonkwo's friend is portrayed as a level-headed, confident family man and one of the enduring leaders of his clan? We see Obierika's children--male and female under the umbrella of filial love and unintimidating guidance, engaging in the perpetuating process of getting married, having children and winning wrestling matches (50; 114-123). On the other hand, the name "Okonkwo" has an intimidating sound which creates a picture of erratic tension and precipitous temperament. In its uncorrupted form, "Oke-nkwo", the name signifies a male born on Nkwo market day. In its corrupted form the name "Oko-nkwo" has become in recent time a stock parlance used in jest to connote a male of irrational size and impulsive behavior. Anyone who reads *Things Fall Apart* in the light of the above insight on Igbo nomenclature would readily observe that Okonkwo's deportment in the novel is in character. One thing that should be stressed here is that Achebe's naming of his hero is not accidental. Achebe's intention in his characterization of Okonkwo is to create a fictional figure whose exaggerated notion of maleness and confounding zest for success at any cost would ultimately be his demise. In other words, the author might be warning his country men and women, in particular, and his readers in general, that "they lose it that buy it with much care."

So, unlike his friend Obierika whose home is a sustaining oasis of cultural growth and loyalty, and whose presence is a reassuring beacon of inspiration for his children, Okonkwo's "heavy hand" and "fiery temper" keep his wives and children in constant fear (14). His beating of his wife, Ojiugo during the Week of Peace and thus violating a cultural taboo (30); his impulsive shooting of his second wife, Ekwefi (41); his cutting down [killing] of Ikemefuna, the boy who called him father (59, 60, 63); his loss of his son, Nwoye to the missionaries (157), are actions traceable to Okonkwo's bloated idea of manhood.

As if implying that a brave soldier is one who survives to tell his story, Achebe makes Obierika a survivor in the novel. It is Obierika who confronts his friend, Okonkwo for taking part in the killing of the boy entrusted to his care; it is he who oversees Okonkwo's transition to exile and tries in vain to bridle his frontal attacks on the missionaries after his return to Umuofia. It is Obierika who calmly and fearlessly confronts the District Commissioner in the final drama of the novel in these terms: "That man was one of the greatest men in Umuofia. You drove him to kill himself; and now he will be buried like a dog . . ." (214) To conclude this passage, it is pertinent for us to observe that Obierika's continued presence in *Things Fall Apart* is glaringly functional--to muffle any inclination on the part of the reader to regard Okonkwo as a typical Igbo man. "If he had been," said Gerald Moore, "his example would have been followed by others." Moore is right in maintaining that, "it is Obierika who really represents the most typical role." He sees Okonkwo as "a sort of super-Igbo; and exaggeration of certain qualities admired by his people, but at the expense of others which a rounded man is expected to possess" (127). Obiechina in underscoring the same point, warns that, "It is a mistake to regard Okonkwo as a representative figure whose likes and dislikes represent those of the race" (92).

Another interesting contrapuntal characterization in *Things Fall Apart* is that of Akunna, an Umuofia elder and Mr. Brown, the white missionary. Their unyielding dialectical disputation over God and religion powerfully ridicules the illusion and ignorance of the European colonists, who detractively proclaimed that the African first heard of religion and god from the Europeans. As Achebe, in the words of Jonathan Peters, "had a consciously educational motive in mind when he wrote *Things Fall Apart*" (96), it will be illuminating for us to hear these two men's dialectical fireworks:

> "You say that there is one supreme God who made heaven and earth," said Akunna on one of Mr. Brown's visits.
>
> We also believe in Him and call Him Chukwu. He made all the world and the other gods."
>
> "There are no other gods," said Mr. Brown. "Chukwu is the only God and all others are false. You carve a piece of wood . . . and you call it a god. But it is still a piece of wood."
>
> "Yes," said Akunna. "It is indeed a piece of wood. The tree from which it came was made by Chukwu, as indeed all minor gods were. But He made them for His messengers so that we could approach Him through them . . ."
>
> "You said one interesting thing," said Mr. Brown. "You are afraid of Chukwu. In my religion Chukwu is a loving Father and need not be feared by those who do his will."
>
> "But we must fear Him when we are not doing His will," said Akunna. And who is to tell His will? It is too great to be known." (185-187)

According to Achebe's prefix to the above religious dialectics, "Neither of them succeeded in converting the other but they learned more about their different beliefs" (185). What makes Akunna and Reverend Brown's face-off more impressive is that it is done on an equal and non-subservient footing. Any reader--African or others who encounter characters like Obierika, Ezeudu, Akunna, and even the tragic Okonkwo with impartial candor, would readily affirm that Achebe has lived up to his dictum that, "The writer cannot expect to be excused from the task of re-education and regeneration that must be done" (G.D. Killam 4). Through these noble personages, *Things Fall Apart* has effectively "challenged the colonist's image of the African as a dancing child-minded savage" (*Homenews* 11).

Works Cited

Achebe, Chinua. *Things Fall Apart*. New York: Astor-Honor, Inc. 1959.

Killam, G. D. ed. *African Writers on African Writing*. Evanston: Northwestern University Press, 1973.

Moore, Gerald. *Seven African Writers*. London: Oxford University Press, 1962.

Obiechina, Emmanuel. *Culture Tradition and Society in the West African Novel*. London: Cambridge University Press, 1975.

Oguibe, Olu. "Chinua Achebe: Eagle On Iroko," *Nigeria: Homenews*. Volume 1, No. 18, February 8-14, 1990, page 11.

Palmer, Eustace. *An Introduction to African Novel: A Critical Study*. New York: African Publishing Corporation, 1972.

Peters, Jonathan. *A Dance of Masks: Senghor, Achebe, Soyinka*. Washington, D.C.: Three Continent Press, 1978.